Sandi

Roy

Gaining a org
last chapter.
Way you end.

Question,
what does it feel
like in your body

ask your
heart's wisdom
surrender
reverence
moving from spirit

Praise for The Liminal Odyssey
The Alchemical Power of the Spaces In-Between

"We, as humanity are at a cross-roads. There is an urgency that requires each and every one of us to hold a sacred responsibility to become a practitioner of balance and to accept our role in ushering in a world of feminine agility and wisdom. *The Liminal Odyssey* is infused with the spirit of the feminine and Sande shows us, through her own personal stories and collection of ideas and methods, the practical wisdom we can each apply to our own life's journey."

~Grandmother Flordemayo
Founding Member of the 13 Indigenous Grandmothers
and Founder of The Path

"Everyone has a unique story known only to them that when shared is a sacred gift to the world. In her book, *The Liminal Odyssey*: The Alchemical Power of The Spaces In-Between, Sande Hart's life experiences flow authentically onto the page and reveal her own dance within her own sacred liminal space. From her sobering and chilling experience, visiting Auschwitz and Birkenau death camp, to her cry out to the stadium-filled crowd to save an abandoned dog, Sande captures and shares many life lessons that evoked inspiration, and at times melted me into a sacred surrender to truths I had only known unconsciously."

~Clay Boykin
Circles of Men Project and The New Compassionate Male

"As Sande's "frequency editor" it has been a delight to walk with her on her Liminal Odyssey as she light-heartedly, poetically and profoundly guides her readers into the magic that awaits us all in the frequency of trust. She leads us into the time-out-of-time where we learn to allow synchronicities to weave a tapestry from the many threads of our lives into living our bliss here and now. Our awareness expands, our hearts open, and we walk through life with ease, grace and abundance. This book is a precious gem to be experienced from many perspectives as Sande drops breadcrumbs to nourish us on our own odyssey to realizing our highest potential."

~Connie Baxter Marlow, Co-Author: *The Trust Frequency: Ten Assumptions for a New Paradigm,* Facilitator: *The Dance of Souls: The Relationship (R)Evolution*

"Insight is wisdom when it inspires you to seek the potential within yourself. Sande Hart's book, *The Liminal Odyssey,* provides you with an invitation to discover the threshold within you that gives profound meaning to your life, even within this crazy world. She entices you into her world of discoveries, and as you laugh and cry, you soon find you want to live in the kind of alchemical reality that she knows intimately well. It's a book you won't want to put down and you'll want to keep handy on your bookshelf for those moments when you aren't sure what to think or do next. Flip it open to a random page and get a burst of wisdom that will guide and embolden you to live, as the author suggests, in epic proportions."

~Misa Hopkins, best-selling author, The Root of All Healing, and the Sacred Feminine Awakening series

"*The Liminal Odyssey* pulsates with Sande Hart's relentless courage to position herself on the delicate threshold between crisis and action as she explores how best to fulfill her life mission as an interfaith leader and champion of rights for women and girls worldwide. In her touching vulnerability, she grants us access not only to her hopes and dreams, but also to her crises of confidence. She gives generous credit to time-honored sources of wisdom and the inspiring individuals she met along the way, but ultimately, she returns to the sacred golden threshold, the liminal holding place, where anything and everything is possible. Read her compelling story!"

~Ruth Broyde Sharone, Interfaith Leader
and Creator of INTERFAITH: The Musical

"The human adventure is an evolutionary journey filled with challenges and unknowns. In transitional times such as these, many of us long for a mentor, someone to take us by the hand and whisper reassurance that, despite outward appearances, everything is unfolding exactly as it must. And fortunately, every so often, a guidebook comes along to provide a map of the territory ahead. Sande Hart's *Liminal Odyssey* is such a book. It will provide you with the vision and the courage and the confidence to go where the brave dare not go, and to emerge transformed, your butterfly wings spread wide."

~Andrew Cameron Bailey, co-Author of *The Trust Frequency: Ten Assumptions For A New Paradigm*. Author of *The Mayflower Revelations*

"Sande Hart shows us how to live our lives as a Liminal Odyssey. Looking deeply into the experiences life brings us and connecting the dots yields a rich and meaningful life. There are no ordinary lives seen through the lens Sande has discovered through her own personal Liminal Odyssey. Read this book and you will see your own life in an entirely different way."

~Patricia Fero LMS, Author of *What Happens When Women Wake Up?*, *Sacred Marching Orders*, and *What Happens When Women Converge*

"Becoming present, listening to our inner wisdom, is a key element in *The Liminal Odyssey*. Paying attention, listening with wonder and curiosity, noticing the mystery and magic of life, resting in silence are practices to guide your experience as you read this book of awakening."

~Kay Lindahl, The Sacred Art of Listening and Founder of The Listening Center

"Poise at a threshold, with the agility of a clear, conscious mind and an open-heart center, is an act of bravery and courage. With characteristic authenticity, Sande invites us to share her Liminal Odyssey, the very definition of surprise moments on the precipice. Enchanting!"

~Dr. Nancy Gahles, Health and Harmony Wellness Center

The Liminal Odyssey

THE ALCHEMICAL POWER OF THE SPACES IN-BETWEEN

The Liminal Odyssey
The Alchemical Power of The Spaces In-Between

Copyright by Sande Hart 2022

Registered with the Library of Congress

All rights reserved.
No part of this book may be used or reproduced in any manner whatsoever without written permission.

Cover Art
Luna So-Lar Tara
by Katherine Skaggs

ISBN: 9798799180546

I dedicate this book to the dog.

Contents

Giving Thanks and Gratitude i
Foreward v
An Invitation ix
Introduction xiii

1. **What About the Dog?** 1
   The Sacred Art of Listening For The Call 7
2. **Grandmother's Wisdom** 11
   Timefulness 15
3. **Devastating Grace** 19
   Forgiveness, Sacrifice and Bliss 27
4. **The Mother of (All Nations) Invention** 33
   We Are Nature 45
5. **Timeful Re-Union** 53
   Sacred Cultivating of Synchronicities 57
6. **Sacred Enoughness and the Red Tent** 63
   Meeting Your Maiden, Mother, Crone 67
7. **Abracadabra: The Sacred Integrity of Our Creation** 75
   Impeccability and Grace 80
8. **Heart-Shaped Evidence** 83
   The Trust Frequency 88
9. **Intergenerational Trauma and the Angel Corp** 93
   Our Ancestors, Allies and Angels 95
10. **Self-Realization and The Sacred Agreement** 99
    Mind Over Matter to The Power of You 107
11. **Dear Linda** 115
    Fulfilling Your Planetary Assignment with Courage 120
12. **Acorn Rain in Birkenau** 123
    Being The Sacred Gardener 127

Appendices

Epilogue.. 129
A Note From The Editor... 131
A Reference Guide.. 133
Chapter Symbols... 137
References 139
About the Author..141

Giving Thanks and Gratitude

"If the greatest prayer you ever say is thank you, it will be enough."
~Meister Eckhart

"Thank you" is insufficient, even if it were the highest prayer, to express my gratitude to the following people. I also know that behind each one is a story that led them into my life, and an individual or two to thank whom I will never meet. I can draw a line of connectivity between each of the following allies on my Liminal Odyssey to demonstrate how each could be recognized for leading me to the other. Each is an essential pearl on my Indra's Net.

Charlon Bobo- this prayer of giving thanks will surely be insufficient to fully express my indebtedness to you. Because I know you can decipher the code of the energy in every sentence, I will try. Your transformational inspiration, wisdom, and mystically keen editorial skills leave me breathless. You have held this book's life in your hands and cared for her as if she were your own. Your sculpting finesse is rooted in your ability to let go, and with a non-dualistic unattachment. Because of that, I could put a name to this ideology and tell my story with grace. Within every step, you have ensured I was in my integrity so that the spirit of this writing would be authentic. I will forever be soaking in the 5-D sensory experience you have guided me into.

Jean Shinoda Bolen- your exploration of liminal space was the missing piece to a puzzle I hadn't realized I was constructing until you provided the framework for it. It would not be the first journey you have either affirmed, inspired, and/or taught me, and certainly will not be the last. Your trust that I expand this concept of liminal space with integrity is humbling. Thank you for blowing your dandelion in my direction. You have entrusted and cheered me on to carry out this concept into the world through my storytelling. How will I ever be complete in thanking you?

Linda Cerny- my living diary since seventh grade—we have been blessed with a unique relationship that is like no other. You have afforded me nearly 50 years of unwavering friendship, sisterhood, accountability, love, and writing experience. Thank you for the practice

Cynthia and David Lundin- thank you for providing me a nurturing nest where I would begin and finish this book; a sanctuary nestled on the very cliffs where my toes once dangled, where my roots and my story began, and the place that has enculturated my life. I am forever grateful for your love, friendship, and house keys.

Cindy- from our aimless walks around PV in wraparound maxi skirts while looking for innocent adventures, you have shown me how to see the silly truth in every little thing for the past 44 years. Because of you, I learned to see things through the lens of their ridiculous nature, and to lighten up.

Patricia Fero- your mentorship, support, and pom-poms have been there for me constantly urging me to follow my *Yes*, right into the pages of writing this book. In fact, I am confident I would not have a book to thank you and the others in had it not been for your encouragement, "magical" connection, and support. You are a model of humility and reverent listening. As you frame it in your book, *What happens When Women Converge,* you create an environment where "essence to essence" relationships can thrive.

Emily Hart, Patrick Hart, Connie Baxter Marlow, Andrew Cameron Bailey, Tami Sheik, Christine Denari, Linda Cook, Rose Tanaglia, and Ruth Broyde Sharone- you all showed up as midwives of the birthing of this book by giving me your advice and your loving, critical eyes in the spirit of trust. I am better because of you.

My too-many-to-name S.A.R.A.H. Sisters who have shown me what generosity of joy looks and feels like. I have been on the receiving end of your crone wisdom, laughter, support, connections, and Love. Out of the clouds you came, even when I did not know I needed you. Your wisdom, gifts, and direction are awe-inspiring and not a single treasure has gone unnoticed and/or unapplied.

Marcia Floyd- the matriarch of my sisters whose maternal love for me has been an anchor in my life.

To the following whose work, a product of your soul's purpose, has informed mine- There are not enough words to express my gratitude for your life's journey so that I could make sense of what I can now call a *Liminal Odyssey*. I bow deeply to Joseph Campbell, Dr. Riane Eisler, Rabbi Dr. Tirzah Firestone, Kay Lindahl, Gary Zukav and Linda Frances, Sister/Brother/Chief Phil Lane, Jr., Dr. James Doty, Dr. Bruce H. Lipton PhD, Dr. Nina Meyerhof, Clay Boykin, Rabbi Allen Krause, Grandmother Flordemayo, Great Grandmother Mary Lyons, Kathryn Lohre, Masami, Hiro and the Saionji family, Ruth Broyde Sharone, Leland Stewart, "Batman" Tom and Sheila Thorkelson, Deborah Moldow, Katherine Skaggs, Paramahansa Yogananda, Greg and his brother, and the dog.

Connie Baxter Marlow and Andrew Cameron Bailey- alone you are masters in your unique work. Together you are a collective force and gift from the center of the Universe. Both your friendship and your book, *The Trust Frequency*, continue to transform my life. Your subtle but mighty advice and recommendations on this project transformed my writing, and I expect it will do the same for my readers' lives. You took ample time with me to ensure the energy of this book was in its highest of frequencies and we are all better because of it.

Connie- you have provided *The Liminal Odyssey* with an additional and rare kind of editing, one that transcends the cosmetic and structural modifications, by breathing into the pages a frequency in the integrity of trust and universal truth. That truth reverberates throughout the pages, like a pebble in a pond. Thank you for being this book's "Frequency Editor."

Katherine Skaggs- It's as if my angels sent for you before this work was complete because they knew it would not be without you. Your generosity and gifts of your *Mythical Goddess Tarot* deck, and your book *Artist Shaman Healer Sage* received midway through this writing, made it necessary to create an additional chapter. But you were not done yet. Then you created Luna Sol-Lar Tara, the magical image that caught my eye and my heart. It was as if you created her especially for this book's cover. Knowing the spirit in which you create, wrapping up these pages in a cover that was painted in a sacred manner makes this book sacred.

To everyone whom I have seen through the eyes of victimhood, suffering, hurt, and abandonment, I thank you for forcing me onto a new path and the opportunity to "feel all the feels," practice discernment, and the value of being authentic and in integrity with whom I call into my circle. I am grateful for you.

I am grateful to the one who pointed out my errors, doubts, fear, neuroses, obsessions, and the shadow side of every thought. Doughty Dora was on my heels and irritating my senses until I saw my own light. The Divine Ms. D. has served me well.

Thank you to my angels and ancestors, who are in some cases, one and the same. Your wisdom, signs, and loving web in the form of a protective harness have successfully kept me safe. May my life be a blessing to your life of suffering, joys, love, and hope.

To my dear reader, this book has written me, with you as my ally, in gratitude and humility that a fellow adventurer was reading these words, keeping me focused on integrity, Love, and imagining a new reality born of wonderment and joy for you.

For my children Emily and Matthew, and my "McKids" Shane and Kaitlin, my grandchildren Wyatt and Holiday, and the next 7 generations, it is you who gave me motherhood, made me a Bubby, mother-in-law, and show me who I am every day. I can't wait to find out what you will teach me next.

To the one whom I prayed for so hard, who blows in my sails, has put me on planes to faraway places making every opportunity available, and who listens me into a condition of discovery and disclosure, he who has created a safe and loving home for me, Emily and Matthew, a plethora of dogs and one 17-year-old goldfish. You've gifted us all a space that is full of love, laughter, patience and given me a name I am proud to spell in the shape of a heart. Thank you, Patrick. My prayers were answered.

Foreword

Sande Hart's master opus touches the soul as she reveals her life experiences by diving deeply into her multifaceted process of questioning everything and releasing all preconceived societal ideas. Sande commits to living life by listening carefully to the gifts laid at her feet, even and especially when they are an uncomfortable teaching. She commits continually to evolving her spiritual conscious awareness towards a condition of bliss. *The Liminal Odyssey* stands out as an authentic tale that invites us to identify and dig into our own story to understand ourselves as well as our soul's desires. Sande's *What About The Dog* story is an amazing tale of synchronistic inspiration and initiates her journey, followed by a conceptual framework, inviting us to alchemize our life's pilgrimage, and what we must leave behind in order to actualize a life in full integrity. The book may be considered a roadmap of how to traverse the stop and go signs, slow down to the sound of our heart's wisdom, and become its sacred gardener.

Congratulations Sande. With clarity and sincerity, you open your heart and mind, inviting us into your exploration for focused purpose to alchemize our own journey, until it becomes an Odyssey.

So, how did I come to this understanding so I could walk along the side of Sande? As an educational practitioner, having directed ten schools district in Vermont, operated a children's farm camp, as well as having traveled and worked in over 100 countries, I know we must educate our children to awaken their evolved and authentic life's potential. We are at the threshold of transitioning out of the industrial and technological era into the spiritual dimension of understanding the framework of wholistic thinking and behaving. If we are to do justice to this future, then we must become aware that the times are changing and to change with them. The current and future generations depend on us to upscale our behaviors and embrace a new way of thinking.

Each generation has the capability of becoming more conscious and closer to furthering our own evolution. No longer do we need to imitate what has come before us, but to take a chance and stretch the edges of our preconceived notions of the universal laws of life. We need a new narrative. We are creating our children's history, and since they are fully impressionable to their parents, elders and teachers, who else then should consider learning new ways of relating and imagining our outcomes? Since those outcomes impact our children, whose minds are already seeded with higher consciousness, do they need more from the past behaviors, or to be exposed to new styles? With every breath, we can shift the definition of success from professional aspirations and money in the bank, to the freedom to make satisfying personal choices with integrity for the betterment of the whole world.

It behooves each one of us to realign our ethical and moral compass away from culture of domination and suppression. It is our moral duty to alter our mind's perceptions and begin to rewire our belief system of the way things were. We will never go back to the past and we can only build the future based on our present thinking. So how do we create this new "present?" When we consciously and consistently behave in accordance with our highest and deepest value system, it becomes our reality. Culturally, when two or more agree on a reality, then that becomes a truth. According to many of the world's doctrines, if ten percent of the world's population hold the same view, that becomes the new world, it becomes the reality. How are you contributing to the new reality?

After the Covid pandemic and climate crisis are behind us, and that day will come, we will be better equipped to recognize that we are all part of one human species, interrelated and interdependent on one other in a culture of harmony, because we are living our authentically impeccable life. *The Liminal Odyssey* takes us there.

Time is of the essence. Take Sande's book and use it as a guide. Consider this one of the most important lessons you will receive in life as a key to the mysteries of how to become a spiritual activist and feeling joyfully free. There is so much confusion in the world, everything is unsettled, thus up for grabs.

Now the time. Like an acorn ready to sprout an entire forest, take a lead so the emergent seedlings of new life for our planet will grow. This has happened before and is calling us now. Do you hear this calling? Go forth and carry this inside yourself. The world is evolving, are you?

If Sande's book is to touch anyone, then it is to understand and practice the steps to cultivate internal freedom as a spiritual cornerstone of how to live life akin to a world that works for everyone. Each person who takes this seriously will see how the steps are broken down to fortify a process, giving credit to its respectful teacher and further creating an interdependent and multidimensional tool kit to navigate our daily life. These practices are inherent in Sande's process and can be personalized by any person reading this book. Take this one step at a time. Take this seriously. Work on it like your life depended on it. It does!

-Dr. Nina Meyerhof, EdD
One Humanity Institute and Children of the Earth

Dr. Nina Meyerhof is one our world's most dynamic visionary peacemakers. She transcends what is traditional with an eye on shifting a culture towards the human potential of conscience evolution. She leads with a playful heart that is authentic, and a wisdom that is awe-inspiring.

Nina has made a life of advocating for children and youth because she knows our future depends on their well-being and wholeness. She is an innovative educator who is committed to global responsibility through authentic learning. She is the Co-Founder of Children of The Earth and The One Humanity Institute.

Nina is the recipient of The Mother Theresa Award, The Public Peace Prize, The Citizen's Department of Peace Award, The International Educators Award for Peace and is the co-author of *Conscious Education: The Bridge to Freedom*

An Invitation

If we look at the path, we do not see the sky.
We are Earth people on a spiritual journey to the stars.
Our quest, our Earth walk is to look within to know who we are
to see that we are connected to all things,
that there is no separation.
Only in the mind.

~Native American Proverb Source Unknown

This book is a multi-disciplinary and fun-filled exercise into the journey of our life with the intent that we do not miss mundane treasures, not-so-secret passage doors, or expansive opportunities meant to be ours.

Please, question everything you read in this book with careful discernment. I don't take anyone's word for anything. It is not so much out of a lack of trust, but a different sort of judgment; one that requires my own truth, wisdom, and gut approval.

Should you accept this mission, this book could serve as a suggestive manual to get there, but it is more of a true-blue account and the applications of measures and weights bestowed upon me from a combination of world-renowned thought leaders, teachers, those I thought were my arch nemeses, and, of course, my angels, told through actual, often wildly synchronistic experiences in my life, which I, in full vulnerability, share with you.

Yet, above all the external factors and influences is an innate sense I learned to hone, through my own personal cleansing process of which I had to find another word. *Journey* was just not cutting it, and, in that search, I came upon a realization of something I could not find in the world, so I wrote it here for myself. And, if I may be so humbly bold, I invite you to join me in the exploration.

I am even so daring as to suggest this is a new theory, one I call a *Liminal Odyssey*. But even as I write the word *new*, I figure this is just an idea that has been floating in the Universe, waiting to bump into, and burrow into someone who was a perfect specimen, with a combination of life experiences, suffering, wild adventures, and insight; one who feels this exploration is a bigger responsibility to ride and/or follow until it becomes meaningful.

Once it identified me as a ripe recipient, it picked up speed and accelerated in my direction. As this concept was hurtling through space, it collected particles of other philosophies and wisdom from those I have had the privilege to bump into in my life so far. The moment it hit me, it appeared as a familiar feeling. It was equally satisfying, like the feeling you get when placing the last piece into a puzzle, creating a complete picture.

I have yet to get to all the corners of my psyche to say I am squeaky clean and crystal clear, without shadows and fault lines. Like the art form Kintsugi, when the cracks and fault lines are alchemized with pure gold, the vase is not only stronger than the original but also far more beautiful than any artist could have planned.

I invite you to dance, grapple, and wrestle with this theory. If the message agitates you or delights your senses, wonder why. The moment you do, you are in a liminal space. What you do next will determine your Liminal Odyssey.

Throughout this book, you'll find references to the biology of an assigned-at-birth woman. While I refer to archetypal essentialism based on the biological cycles of the female body, I am sensitive to those who may not identify as a woman or identify without innate physiology. As such, I invite you to consider these references as nothing more than symbolic pillars of an evolution of personal growth, no matter how you identify, or if you identify at all. Be assured, that has no bearing on applying the Liminal Odyssey to your life.

An Invitation

A Message from the Thirteen Indigenous Grandmothers

"As you move through these changing times… be easy on yourself and be easy on one another. You are at the beginning of something new. You are learning a new way of being. You will find that you are working less in the yang modes that you are used to.

You will stop working so hard at getting from point A to point B the way you have in the past, but instead, will spend more time experiencing yourself in the whole, and your place in it.

Instead of traveling to a goal out there, you will voyage deeper into yourself. Your mother's grandmother knew how to do this. Your ancestors from long ago knew how to do this. They knew the power of the feminine principle… and because you carry their DNA in your body, this wisdom and this way of being are within you.

Call on it. Call it up. Invite your ancestors in. As the yang-based habits and the decaying institutions on our planet begin to crumble, look up. A breeze is stirring. Feel the sun on your wings."

Introduction

The first time I heard the word *liminal* was from author Jean Shinoda Bolen, who describes it by its Latin root, "threshold," the space in-between crisis and action. In that space, we can interpret, examine, dream, and imagine possibilities for new creativity that is so necessary right now to move on from old problems, beliefs, and myths of who we are. The space in-between is the demarcation place of a paradigm shift. It occurs after the separation of what was and before what is and can determine what will be. However, one need not experience a crisis to drop into the liminal space. In fact, I find opportunities all day long.

Tokens, secret doorways, and pearls of wisdom fall at our feet on our life's journey. Yet, if we dismiss them as mundane or inconsequential, we may be forced onto a sometimes-arduous path until we can no longer step over them because they are ours to pick up. In a Liminal Odyssey, those gems become life-sized, and we can no longer ignore them.

The origin of the game Chutes and Ladders dates back to the 2nd Century AD, named *Moksha Patam*, translating to *Snakes and Ladders*. It is a game of chance where we find ourselves facing an opportunity to take a path to a higher level of awareness and meaning or, we may find ourselves on a seemingly easy slide downhill but missing a potentially exciting game. Unlike this game of chance, we have choice, and we can cultivate the skills and habits to choose the ladder with every breath. My personal ladders elevated me into hearty adventures that led me to a fortune at the bottom of a box of cigarettes and a Holocaust death camp.

According to the theories of The Hero's Journey, founded on philosophies of Carl Jung and popularized by Joseph Campbell and Walt Disney, we move through a variety of stages, like building blocks, one stage preceding the other, in a seemingly predictable series of events and an obstacle course of rivers to traverse and tall buildings to climb, and sometimes, doing all of that in a hailstorm.

Just look at any fantasy movie. We can count on obvious and camouflaged wizards to point us in the right direction, and always a number of antagonists and lovable yet mischievous pixies to trip us up. We experience a series of challenges and grow with more character and our true archetypal identity. Only after we have slain the dragons and learned from our stumbles do we get the happy ending, or not, but regardless, we made it to the end of our story. The plots are the same and apply whether our life's a mystery, comedy, action thriller, or courtroom drama.

These Journeys are illustrated in a straight line, a circle, or even a spiral, but respectfully, both the Hero's and Heroine's Journeys missed the mark for me. The same may be true for you. Indeed, these well-documented and challenged philosophies have merit. Both are necessary, and yet there's so much more, which is where we enter The Liminal Odyssey.

The Hero's Journey is important to understand so we can identify the signposts, as if they are county line markers confirming our coordinates in life, but they do not always show up in a linear fashion as found when looking down on a map. This is where we need a new structure, or better yet, drop the confines of what's predictable and start looking up for what wants to emerge as the new archetypal being co-creating a new myth. It is birthing in each of us right now.

Being willing to read the map to know where we are is affirming and can also be a lifeline. But, like any map, it never shows us the culture of the area we may be passing through. We could assume, based on topography, structures, and outward appearances, that it is definitely a place we want to race through or aspire to live in one day, but what if we were to miss a hidden goldmine or priceless piece of porcelain? It's up to us to pull into those spaces, walk up to a door and peek inside the cupboards.

The following is a common template of the Hero's Journey, based on research of a variety of interpretations of Joseph Campbell's philosophy, and inspired by Carl Jung.

Introduction

1. Call to action, sometimes met with refusal until it cannot be ignored. Sometimes not recognized at all but inspires a shift of perception and/or action
2. Assistance shows up in the form of mentors or wizards
3. Departure, crossing the line of no-return
4. Trials, tests, meeting monsters and alligators
5. Approaching or meeting one's higher self-potential
6. New crisis or ordeal
7. Discovery of your treasure or reward
8. Return to a happy, better life or resurrection of clarity
9. Resurrection, Resolution, and Contentment

The Hero's Journey can run the span of a lifetime, be experienced in chunks of time, or in a momentary situation. As previously mentioned, it is also a solid template for most motion pictures.

To discount it as a "Journey" feels way too narrow and topical, missing altogether the depth, breadth, and alchemical magic of its power, and opportunity of the spaces in-between. While Joseph Campbell brilliantly takes us into the myths and cultural significance of a Hero's Journey as a path, I had to apply the skills and tools to build capacity in-between the steps on my path so they were meaningful in real-life applications.

Joseph's greatest advice is to follow your bliss. This was the very guidance I went looking for when I found The Hero's Journey years ago. As I looked back and charted my own journey thus far, I noticed patterns in synchronicities that were evidence of something mystical, magical, and the stuff of which myths are made.

These moments-of-chance were far from the mundane experience I discounted them to be at the time. I discovered that those moments of insignificance were really *in-significance.* After closer examination, I began to notice that the essential elements in the form of skills I had learned through each story along the way created a powerful and complementary collection.

Each chapter is in two parts, the true story followed by the skill, tools, and lessons cultivated.

Alone, each skill is its own body of work with its own planet of research and expertise based on a variety of well-respected and researched disciplines, methods, traditions, physics, models, and science. Yet, when applied together, they create a constellation, where collectively their own unique rotations create a gravitational pull that provides conditions for a system that moves us toward bliss. You will find each of these in this book, assigned to their respective experience, and framed by The Hero's Journey. I call this expedition toward the universe of bliss *The Liminal Odyssey*.

The Liminal Odyssey is what happens when we make an experience an experiment. As I started to apply the Liminal Odyssey to my life, I began to connect more pearls, discovered new insights, and noticed more allies that came both as fairy godmothers and those cloaked as unsavory characters recognizable in any play.

Soon, the Odyssey experience not only multiplied, it accelerated zero-to-warp-speed, often in a blink of the eye. From the very beginning, this book lived me, breathed me, and wrote me. Many of the discoveries happened after I was well into the writing process, making it necessary to add a chapter or two. The Liminal Odyssey will never stop producing more, "Aha's" and experiences of clarity and resurrection of the moment it follows and will until my last moment and breath. This is my same wish for you.

As I stepped back and looked at that new pattern through my wild life experiences, its shape was something bold, large and in-charge. [Double snap here.] I put it in the petri dish, shared it with some friends who became my gift of a real-life proof of concepts, and voila, it's here for you now to pull apart, examine, and dance with.

Because this is a multi-disciplinary experience, I spend some time on the various methods and philosophies, but you are encouraged to dive deeper into what calls to you. You will certainly add your own ingredients because you have lived an adventure-full life too, and those unique skills that work for you have a home in this constellation. My hope is that you recognize the power of the confluence of tools you have picked up, by what you discover in this book, through your own research, and through the culture you were raised in that comprises a customized toolkit to excavate, chart, and light up the life you have the privilege of living. May that toolkit continue to expand and fill with even more instruments of discovery for the rest of your life.

Indra's Net (Indra is King of the Heavens in Buddhist philosophy and derived from the Sanskrit word indrajwāla) is of infinite proportions spanning the vastness of the universe. Comprised of universal geometric patterns, each meeting point is supported by a pearl of wisdom, a life lesson, and luminous reflection. Its grace suspends in the space of our lives and its threads, our storylines, are connected by droplets of nutrient-rich pools for us to reflect upon.

My greatest fear has been to live a safe and mundane life, failing to leave behind meaningful pearls in the shape of stories, accomplishments, and wild adventures my grandchildren can brag about, definitely be inspired by, and hopefully learn from. Maybe my stories will appear in their lives as a pearl on their net.

What if we expect that each mundane situation or environment to be nothing more than an invitation, a challenge to be stretched beyond its outward appearance through simple curiosity that may create a pearl? What if we did not ignore the catalyzing sense of creativity, spontaneity, and action we feel in our body when that moment comes? Or maybe it just deserves a little gratitude to alchemize the gift it is. What matters most is paying attention to the Odyssey's gifts.

It is in that attention we can begin to connect the threads and pearls of those experiences, yet the patterns will surprise you. The storyline of one's life often zigs and zags, seemingly with no sense of connectedness. That is until we listen closely to the soundtrack in the background and follow the threads of the clues and tokens of wisdom along the path. Without fail, the threads connect. When the storyline is examined more closely, one will find a magical mystery tour complete with all the fixings of adventure, mayhem, trauma-induced growth, joy, heartache, and immeasurable blessings. It's messy. And therein lies the environment of The Liminal Odyssey (as well as any good Pixar film.)

Required for admission into that place is to surrender to the God/Spirit-gifted treasures we were entrusted to nurture and protect with our body and our lives and not take a second of it for granted. Therefore, we must trust, just as a caterpillar trusts it's time to cocoon with no expectation or promise of what's on the other side. Only then can she emerge in her highest and most glorious potential. The very act of struggling to climb out of her cocoon gives her the authentic strength and power to do her butterfly work in the world. She must go through the process herself. Yet, unlike the journey of a caterpillar to butterfly, where no one can help her or she will die, we thrive with the support of our allies, those we can see and many we cannot.

We were all born with a life force. It's the invisible hand that instructs our lungs to breathe us and our heart to beat. It instilled the awareness that it was time for the butterfly to come out of her womb and spread her wings. It is in constant motion and manifests in a potentially adventurous journey, but only if the mind's eyes are looking carefully and we are willing to accept challenges and, when necessary, get out of its way, taking time to see the treasures and potentiality. Then we can say with authority that we have accepted the challenge and are on The Liminal Odyssey.

The adventure of the Liminal Odyssey is like the weaving of a web, like an Indra's Net. When we step back, we see a mandala with a sacred center. But look closer and we will see the back and forth, the sacred geometry, and the support system of each new connection point. Each point is dependent upon the whole and required for a maximized lived life where nothing was left unopened, unexamined, or not stretched to its full potential. That point (or pearl) is where the nectar is. We know that each pearl is a bonding agent of stories, allies, and priceless lessons. It's where we grow with more wisdom to strengthen our path onward.

For me, accepting the challenge is not an option, it is a holy responsibility.

Introduction

*"Do not ask your children
to strive for extraordinary lives.
Such striving may seem admirable,
but it is the way of foolishness.
Help them instead to find the wonder
and the marvel of an ordinary life."*

~William Martin

One
What About The Dog?

*Being listened to is so close to being loved that
most people cannot tell the difference.*

~David Augsburger

"It's a hot day and someone left their dog in the car."

100,000 rowdy people were in the stands by 10 AM. The program had yet to begin and within 10 minutes I was swept away, forgetting where I was and what we were meant to do.

It took 35 years to realize this was my call to action, my maiden voyage into the Liminal Odyssey. I heard the call like a bellowing horn. I felt the catalytic shock to my heart. It pushed me back into my seat and I was momentarily blinded by the rush of a holy war's call to action. There is no consideration of what to do next: right or wrong. It was clear. You have no choice in the matter. The 37 trillion cells in your body are committing mutiny on your senses, activating your feet, arms, and voice. You simply jump to attention, pump your first with a rebel yell, with spirit on fire, and lunge forward. Like a marionette being controlled by a higher source, you surrender and say, "YES."

The Liminal Odyssey

On June 6th, 1982, the Rose Bowl in Pasadena was swollen to the max with a reported 100,000 people for a no-nukes rally called Peace Sunday with the vision statement, "We have a dream."

By the looks of it, like me, most came for the line-up of rock stars of everyone relevant since the '60s, most of which were last-minute appearances like Bob Dylan, Bonnie Raitt, Stevie Wonder, Bette Midler, and Fleetwood Mac not even making the original program guide. However, we were called to be there to stop nuclear proliferation, protect our planet and save humanity. Nestled between Woodstock and Live Aid, Peace Sunday invoked the same spirit of a generation who'd had enough, and rock-and-roll speaks our truth to power.

The emcee made the announcement. "...and," she added, "if that is your dog, please go roll down your windows." A collective low-grade boo hushed over the crowd, but the dog was quickly forgotten.

Bands played their sets. Stitched in between instrument breakdowns and setups were statements from speakers, in the form of activists, celebrities, religious and political leaders, and environmentalists who had something to say to impress and implore a crowd of impressionable and stoned concert goers. More bands, more speakers, and the patchwork went on in that manner for 10 hours on a blisteringly hot day. Talk to anyone about that day, and the common memory was that no one brought enough sunscreen.

Not only did I not forget about the dog, I was incensed. I could not think of anything else. I seized the moment. Sitting stage left, in a section not far from the stage, I was sure my voice could be heard. The band completed its short set and the Reverend Jesse Jackson was walking to the mic. It rose in me like a mortal cry, "What About The Dog?" Surely, they could hear me and report back eventually. But it was not enough. I could not be heard but I could not think of anything but the dog. "What about the dog? What about the dog? What about the dog?" I chanted until I was drowned out by Reverend Jackson. Again, my moment came. I started the chant again, and now my three friends joined me. Another opening, another opportunity. More chanting, more drowning out. I did not give up. It did not take long before our entire section was chanting, "What About the Dog?"

What About The Dog?

At the time of incident, the sympathetic nervous system is activated and releases the hormones adrenaline and cortisol, which surge through the body and supercharge courage, and enough muscle strength to lift a Mack truck off a child. The transformation began in my cells. They were rearranging while I was pumping my voice. Decades later, I realized that was the very moment I accepted the challenge on my personal Liminal Odyssey.

While the exact details are fuzzy, throughout the entire day, the entire stadium was chanting, "What about the dog?" every opportunity we had. One detail I am sure of: around 4 PM, as I was walking back into the stadium from the concessions area, I heard it. "What about the dog?" The chant had started without me. *'What had just happened? Had I started a movement? What was it that touched others about the humanity of one dog, in the backdrop of saving all of humanity? Is this how one activates a critical mass?* I wondered.

In Mary Oliver's prayer, *When Death Comes*, she says, "I don't want to end up simply having visited this world." I am hyper-aware that time is fleeting, and I want to backward-plan my life with only one closing element: contentment. Who knows what the trail of adventure leading there will be? If I can leave this place knowing I did not waste a single opportunity to max out every relationship and question mark, "contentment" will be my epitaph. That's frustrating for someone who does not have the resources or know-how to manifest it all, but I can start with "Yes", then follow raw curiosity, even if it seems ridiculous, like chanting four simple words at a no-nukes rally.

In fact, it's those silly little things—like unknowingly catalyzing 100,000 people on a wave of intention—that reverberated throughout my life; it's ever-widening circles rippling around the world through an otherwise missed interconnected storyline that would connect decades later.

Like a wave at any Dodgers game, it only takes two people to start a wave that ripples around the stadium, at least one and a half times. What happened that day was a tsunami where the ever-crashing waves have been knocking me down, picking me up, throwing me in the air, and catching me ever since.

In the book *Blueprint for Revolution: How To Use Rice Pudding, Lego Men, and Other Nonviolent Techniques to Galvanize Communities, Overthrow Dictators, or Simply Change The World*, author Srdja Popovic demonstrates

The Liminal Odyssey

through a series of real-life stories how communities were activated and big problems solved with the most outlandish strategies. In one account, by letting loose a hundred turkeys in a town square, a small group of protestors made the crooked police look ridiculous trying to catch them, only to achieve their goal and get their points across, ultimately healing their civic unrest. Appealing to the critical mass in a creative manner has proven successful and memorable, especially when it includes a dog or some turkeys.

A catalytic shock needn't come in the form of a call to moral action. A catalytic shock may very well be our spirit telling us to be our authentic self in the moment and speak up, release the turkeys, or maybe just dance.

In a quirky homemade video entitled, *Leadership Lessons From The Dancing Guy,* a movement is not necessarily started by the crazy outlier, referred to as the "lone nut" who unapologetically follows his heart or does not question his impulse to express himself in a manner that is rather unconventional and goofy-looking. He is simply moved into action and, as if as natural as taking his next breath, he lunges into the crazy dance, thoroughly relishing his freedom of movement, and his spirit soars. There's no logic, reason, or concern for how he looks to others. He is living large. There was no apology or self-deprivation, even a hint that what he was doing was out of place. It was not expected, and he needn't apologize. In fact, he gives license to the next guy who gets up and dances with him. Now there are two Crazy Dancing Guys, until a swarm of people rush in. Only those standing still on the sidelines are the outliers. Now we have a movement.

But the Crazy Dancing Guy is not the movement leader. It is the First Follower, the one who accepts his outlandish challenge to express himself in the same manner and gives permission, momentum, and a sense of belonging to others to join and create the critical mass.

I know I was the lone nut on that hot Peace Sunday. I do not remember which of my three friends was the First Follower. Next, the small group of people around us rushed in and their collective voice was the momentum necessary, like the activating yeast to my nutty bread.

For the first time in my life, I witnessed the power of my authentic voice; a voice I never had the confidence to hear within myself. Hearing the call

What About The Dog?

to action, and not speaking up was not an option. I planted a bold, unique, and original idea to 100,000 strangers, one at a time, and they agreed with enthusiasm. This is an epiphany I would not realize for several decades, yet at some cellular level, I got it. This was not my last bodacious nutty idea that started a wave. This would be a pattern throughout my life and its power would take me a very long time to harness. As it turned out, I had many more lessons to learn, each threaded together with gossamer threads, seen when I was ready, and if I was willing. Each thread, a story, a journey, often painful, sometimes unbelievable, definitely interesting, and a model Liminal Odyssey.

Had some irresponsible dog owner not left his dog in the car, or some compassionate dog lover, for that matter, not reported it to security, making its way to the emcee and ultimately to my nervous system, it would have been an unremarkably memorable day.

Around 6 PM Bette Midler—another last-minute addition to the line-up—took the microphone and sang *The Rose* a cappella. Before Stevie Wonder could take the stage, the emcee returned to make an announcement. She asked, "SO! You want to know about the dog?" The details are fuzzy, but one thing is clear, she asked the question, the crowd went wild, and then she proclaimed," The dog is fine!" followed by more cheers and random objects flying in the air.

Mr. Wonder was then led to his piano and, in his ever-soft voice, asked for five minutes of silence to pray together. I am not sure which I was more curious about: was I really in the midst of 100,000 otherwise rowdy people who had been in the hot California sun all day, indulging in advocacy-soaked music history, now in a collective silence, or would Mr. Stevie Wonder have gotten five minutes of silence had the emcee not satisfied the big question of the day?

I suspect I was not alone in this mission of the heart, gut, and nervous system. I sense I had a few angels, each with a wicked sense of adventure prodding me to speak up. I always felt accompanied by an angelic support system, but that day I was definitely not alone in my seat. I figured I was still alive at 21 because I had at least a few angels who had my back. I had dodged so many bullets where I could have been kidnapped, slipped off a cliff, thrown in jail, or crashed the car I had stolen from my mom before I knew how to drive. How else did I get this righteous life I strive to maintain while making up for a few poor choices? There is no doubt those dear angels have had their work set out for them since, and they must be exhausted.

Not only do my angels not give up on me, but they also continue to present me with curious experiences soaked in magic, hoping I will pick up on the clues. There must be more than a few. In fact, I am sure I have a full-on Angel Force. Between the platoons of angels pushing me, and squadrons pulling me, there must be twice as many doing double-duty keeping me safe on this Odyssey of the soul; one that took off with a dog locked in a car on a hot day in 1982.

When the fortitude of your internal landscape, activated by a question that demands an answer is stronger than you can ignore, it means this is rightful project to take on, space to fill, door to open or close, and/or your challenge to address and find the solution. You can feel it in your bones when you stop at the threshold of that first realization; a realization that you have a choice. This is the first step on the Liminal Odyssey where you can see a new path. Stepping onto that path means you are willing to listen, an essential element before strategizing your next moves.

To listen another's soul into a condition of disclosure and discovery may be almost the greatest service that any human being ever performs for another.

~Douglas Steere

: separate

The Sacred Art of Listening for The Call

Strengthening the muscle of listening is essential on our Liminal Odyssey. We do this through simple, yet seriously powerful, practices. Awareness and intention for self-realization are our guiding principles. When we set the intention to be true to our authentic selves, then discovery of the self is a joy to uncover. However, seeking it out takes some practice and capacity-building.

Kay Lindahl has been a beacon and model for my community-building work, and who later would become one of my mentors and my friend. She is the founder of *The Listening Center*, a name that conjures up a vision of a place to drive to, an office perhaps, where one can go and practice or learn how to listen. But Kay tells us that it is a space within each of us. It is our center. The place where we remember who we are; where we focus our innermost listening.

Like the title of her book, Kay is a master at the sacred art of listening which she considers a foundational spiritual practice. Kay does not teach us how to listen, but how to prepare to listen, reflect, and be in silence, resulting in presence.

Research shows that we spend close to the entirety of our waking day in communication. We spend 9% writing, 16% reading, 25% speaking, and 50% listening. And two-thirds of the time we spend listening, we are not fully engaged. We usually only remember about half of what we hear, and even that evaporates over time.

While bees, animals, and plant life have sophisticated, innate communication intelligence, we humans are squandering our highly sophisticated gifts. Imagine the depth of relationship with ourselves and others that we are not taking full advantage. Kay shows us the grace of becoming a listening presence, creating a space that opens us up to curiosity, awe, and wonder, invoking an intimacy with others and with our own source/God/Great Spirit. I know this to be true. I have been actively listened to by Kay many times.

Kay was the first to teach me circle principles. Kay identifies 10 Tips for Listening. Three of those skills are: 1; Listen for understanding, 2; Allow a pregnant pause to be sure what was said is honored, and 3; Ask, "Is there anything else that wants to be said?" There almost always is.

I have always found Kay's expertise ideal in not only interpersonal communication but how to listen to oneself to truly know who we are.

If we think we are really paying close attention to our thoughts and our inner words throughout a day, listen up. Only 17% of the day is spent on intentional listening. Imagine what we must be missing, and how inconsiderate and rude to the one we need the most, our self.

The average attention span is about 8 seconds, but we really can't blame ourselves. We have been conditioned by the pace of society, and now technology has accelerated that pace from 0-60 in record time.

When I was a kid, TV commercials were each a few minutes long. Today, the average commercial is 15 seconds, and networks throw 5-15 commercials at us every 10 minutes so we are conditioned to see a lot, very quickly, all the time absorbing how we will be free, authentically happy, and rich if we buy their stuff. We are conditioned to listen to a tsunami of messages at a superficial level and not take a pregnant pause to stop and think, *Hmmm, that's not what I consider authentic happiness*, but plenty of time to remember the phone number. It may not come as a great surprise that media has taught us to be desensitized to our own internal wisdom, but hyper-aware of how to have a better life if we "call right now!"

Also, we have not been educated in the art of listening and mindfulness as pre-school and elementary schools are introducing today. A not-so-recent study found that students taught silence, mindfulness, and meditation, have improved test scores, stopped playground bullying, and retained more information. Kay points out that teaching the practice of silence helps children clear something in themselves that they do not otherwise have the coping skills for. Imagine if the world's nations made this education mandatory for children and adults, including Government 101 classes.

Listening is an art to cultivate, not a passive thing to do. The qualities of practicing an art include being at oneness with our higher self and level of conscientiousness. It's intentional and performed with a sense of purpose, love, and intention. It's a choice we make because it has meaning, and so we embody this art which becomes evident in the outcome. And like any art, it takes practice to cultivate and can be profound to experience by both the artist and the one who experiences its beauty.

Naturally, our ability to listen intentionally rarifies when we meditate, especially through contemplative or mindful meditation practice. But even then, are we really listening our soul into a condition of disclosure and discovery? If we set our intention to that condition, it's a sure bet.

When we are listened to in this spirit, it is truly a gift. I have been in Kay's workshops over the years and a staple in all her presentations is to invite attendees to think about how they felt when they were truly listened to. I needn't write anymore about this practice, but invite you to put down this book, find a piece of paper and write a letter to yourself about that time. When you think you are complete, wait in silence and ask, "Is there anything else that wants to be said? There almost always is.

This is the greatest gift we can ever give to our soul, as this is what the soul desires. When we slow down to the sound of silence, with intention, and are fully present, there is no other. Mystics call this condition ecstasy. Artists call it an aesthetic rapture. I consider it sacred.

Listening to the call means that we are aware of who we are because we can relate with meaning, otherwise, we would not have recognized it in the first place. This is a definition of synchronicity, and I dive into that more in Chapter five, yet not all synchronistic events (which I consider as invitations) are delivered with a hit to the nerve center like my experience at Peace Sunday. Some are faint whispers, easy to ignore. The more we pay attention to them, the more synchronicities we notice and the more obvious and pronounced they become. They can and should be cultivated and sought out. This is what it means to practice the art of listening with intention for self-realization.

Having the intention to practice is only half the equation. Intention's partner is will, which is actually the decision-maker. With the intention and will to listen to the soul, our soul rejoices and becomes more familiar to us, heard more frequently, in louder tones, higher vibrations, and experiences. Our soul rejoices because our recognition of it is its pathway to freedom, and when we use our life to free our soul, we are living into our soul's purpose.

A Liminal Odyssey's qualities of the sacred art of listening, applying intent, taming will, and knowing thyself will ensure a wildly wonder-full and meaning-full life when put into practice.

Two
Grandmother's Wisdom

Whether we jump or are pushed,
or the edge of the known world just crumbles at our feet,
we just fall, spinning into some place new and unexpected.
Despite our fears of falling, the gifts of the world stand by to catch us.

~Robin Wall Kimmerer, *Braiding Sweetgrass*

I was born into an already-established family. My three sisters were ages 9, 11 and 15 with a stay-at-home mom who created a family unit around my father, who had an unpredictable raging temper and always seemed to be disappointed in his life. He had mastered the art of putting on airs for his Lodge brothers and friends. Both my parents excelled in creating a seemingly perfect image for others, caring more about how we looked and what others thought. It was a steadfast and unbreakable rule; pay no attention to your own good sense, feelings, or what is good for you. As long as you look the part, you are safe.

My mom's unexpected pregnancy with me, coupled with my dad's love of the sea, found them looking for a new home and moving to a community in

Palos Verdes, California, called Golden Cove which sits on a peninsula. The foghorn and seabirds were the soundtrack of my life.

Moving to this community meant my mom returning to work, and I was raised by a lumbering Nordic woman we called Dodo. The sun revolved around me at home, and my father and sisters adored me. Over time, dad's business failed, and his health got worse, making his moods even more unpredictable, like a ticking time bomb.

As I got older and everyone started going their own way, leaving me in place, slowly I slipped off my throne as the sparkle in everyone's eyes. My two older sisters moved on with college and/or marriage, leaving me to fend for myself with a sister who hated me for breathing her air. She resented having to stay home and care for me after Dodo was let go.

As time passed, I became a nuisance to my parents and I was alone. I had no guidance, and was not born wired with the capacity to find these things on my own. Or so I thought. Was this my angels' calculated plan to lead me into this journey, having pegged me for someone who, one day would wake up to intestinal fortitude coupled with an awareness of the sacred nature of it all? Was I born with "Spiritual Potential" stamped on my forehead?

Like too many young girls, I had little confidence and managed to slip under everyone's radar for fear of not being enough. I excelled at the art of being invisible. I constructed a story that I was unworthy of love and attention.

I found my solace sitting on the beach watching the waves come and go and come back again, just as they promised. Someone was paying attention to me after all.

As kids, we body surfed and played in the waves for hours, days, and years on end. I was an adult before I realized one of the most profound lessons of my life would come from getting caught and tumbled in the white water.

With little notice, or sometimes out of pure denial of its sheer size and approach, you are forced underwater in a topsy-turvy, disoriented, uncontrollable frenzy. There's no way to know which way is up, and there is nothing to grab to anchor you in place. The only way to manage the turbulent force of nature is to relax and find the ground. There you find calm as the chaos rushes overhead. Then, wait for it all to roll over you, plant your feet and push yourself up through to calm waters. The realization that calm is always underneath the surface is as powerful a lesson as the feeling of ascending back up to where the oxygen is, knowing you will break through the once-turbulent, now residual soapsuds.

Usually, you end up with a crotch full of sand and learn how to remain in the privacy of the water to dump it out so you needn't endure the embarrassment of walking back to your towel carrying a load. Then, you jump back in, knowing it's an adventure and you have the skills to navigate rough waters should you get slammed again, and you know you will if you keep jumping in.

Indigenous culture and I refer to her as Grandmother Ocean. A grandmother's love is unique. It's playful, teeming with life, and full of adventure. It is a rare relationship and one you can trust. She is the ultimate crone.

Perhaps my angels led me to the beach, the far-away kingdom of freedom and trust, showing me that I was acceptable and also able to receive what comes at me, especially if it's a crashing wave. "Just remain calm and sink down. It will definitely pass," is the soothing wisdom I can still hear her whispering in my ear today.

I was gifted this relationship, she and I. She was my second family: the one I chose. She was also my first mentor on my Liminal Odyssey.

I would play in her, she would give me her treasures of sand dollars and seashells, and on occasion, teach me valuable lessons. I promised to never leave her. There's no better sleep than after a full day at the beach, as if she followed me home and cradled me to sleep.

She paid attention to me. Without fail, she offered me the gift in the shape of every tide that rolled in, humbly placing it at my feet and slipping back as if to bow out of the room. I prayed to her and upon her. She is an excellent listener, and if we are patient enough and clear our ego, she will answer our questions, usually pointing out that we had the answers the whole time.

I learned from a friend who is the spiritual leader of the local indigenous tribe how to pray to Grandmother Ocean: "Pick up a stone, any stone and ask your question into it. Then, throw it into the water giving Her your question to answer. Now wait for seven tides to roll in and your answer will come to you."

Depending on the tide, seven waves can either take a very long time, or no time at all, but somehow, the space in between the waves always seem to be voluminous, considerate, as if you can see her thinking and carefully preparing the answer and taking her sweet time. The longer it took for the seventh wave, the more time she knew I needed in those spaces in-between.

In the same way, a Liminal Odyssey is self-defining and based entirely on the time we take in the in-between spaces of our daily lives. Our culture is pretty well versed in being mindful, yet we could learn a thing or two about being timeful. Imagine the reward, a first-class ticket on a space odyssey adventure to the great, wide-open liminality.

> *"The two most powerful warriors are patience and time."*
> -Leo Tolstoy, *War and Peace*

Timefulness

If a Liminal Odyssey requires us to take notice of the moments when we are at the threshold, then understanding timefulness is essential.

About halfway through this writing, I knew I had to speak to Jean Shinoda Bolen. I have known Jean for years, meeting her for the first time at the annual United Nations Commission on the Status of Women in New York. That meeting was not long after I read her book, *Urgent Message from Mother, Gather The Women and Save the World,* which was the first official affirmation that what I was feeling in my bones had merit. While gushing my admiration all over Jean, she stopped me mid-sentence and said, "Do you want to help me?" She then proceeded to fill my pockets with oversized blue buttons announcing her campaign for the U.N. to host a 5th Women's World Conference. In that moment, I witnessed what a crone looks like. (I explore more about this archetype in Chapter six.) Jean was not interested in having her ego fluffed or wasting time on frivolities because she was clear with purpose, following, as she puts it, "her planetary assignment" (or one of them, at least.) So much of Jean's buoyant energy, her books, talks, and presence, along with her introduction to the expression *liminal space* has influenced my life and much of what has since become The Liminal Odyssey.

I sent Jean an email asking to schedule a chat, with a brief description of what I wanted to discuss. I did expect a reply anytime soon, knowing she is very busy. I wanted to tell her a bit about the direction I was taking her philosophy so that I was in complete integrity and not crossing any lines into her work. Within two hours, Jean called me.

I explained how I had stretched the word liminal from a threshold to a gaping space between here and there, the invitation to stay in that space before moving on, and what treasures and opportunities lie in waiting. I also found myself telling her the Peace Sunday story.

She said, and I paraphrase, "Isn't it amazing how while everyone was there for this herculean task of de-escalating nuclear arms and escalating peace on Earth, everyone was able to remember the humanity of one dog." I agreed, and then she said something I had never considered until that moment, "...and seeing themselves as that dog, this unassuming victim of man's quest for power."

Not all realizations are such profound epiphanies. How they get discovered is in liminal space on their own Liminal Odyssey.

Patricia Fero—who has been instrumental in inspiring my writing through her friendship, introductions, mentorship, and her own runway of beautiful books, urged me to ask Jean about Chronos and Kairos time, followed by an insistence to add Jean's book *The Tao of Psychology* to my already impressive collection of Jean Shinoda Bolen books.

Jean explained that ancient Greeks marked time with two systems. Chronos refers to left-brained, scientific with patriarchal tendencies. It is chronological or sequential time. It's quantitative. Kairos is right-brained, creative, playtime and dreamtime. It is a moment of indeterminate time when an incident of significance happens. Aristotle's take is, "Kairos time is the time and space in which the truth will be delivered." It's of a qualitative and permanent nature.

Kairos time is the moment we come to in every one of the stages of The Hero's Journey. At those junctures, whether it's the moment when the call comes in, it's time to get out of Dodge, or we meet our mentors, each test and trial, new crisis or discovery of our treasure, are moments in Kairos time. It's a passing instant that when an opening appears, it must be passed through with intention. It's the timepiece that marks liminal space and invites us to drop into the Liminal Odyssey.

The Integrity of The Potent Spaces In-Between

The Torah: the biblical scrolls containing the first five books of Moses, known as the Jewish Bible or First Testament, and found in every synagogue, is handwritten by a precisely-trained scribe called a *sofer* who studies and practices for years because there can be no mistakes in the ink-quilled text.

In the event of a goof, the process to remove that text is painstaking, and if that word happens to be *God*, the page, parchment that is typically made of a kosher calfskin, is meticulously removed and replaced by hand-stitching and is nothing short of a ritualistic surgery, followed by a ceremonial burial.

Every page has exactly the same number of inches defining its boundaries around the edges of the page and the spaces in between the letters and the words. The scroll is then anchored on each end by an *atzei chaim,* a wooden spindle, which in Hebrew translates to *The Tree of Life.*

If a letter or word becomes faded over time, the scroll must remain closed until the writing is corrected, reminding us that when we lose sight of the holiness in our lives, we need to be timeful for ourselves so that we can find God in those spaces in between *the atzei chaim,* the Tree of Life.

The *sofer* must know more than 4,000 Judaic laws before picking up a quill to write the Torah. I would like to think the reason is, as he is writing the Hebrew letters, he is breathing the laws into that liminal space on the page. Those spaces leave us room to investigate and understand, in our own integrity, what the Torah wants us to know so we are impeccable with our faith. If the words are the intellectual, then the spaces in-between are the spiritual based in Universal law, and we are encouraged to step into that space.

The Japanese concept of *ma* refers to negative space, silence, and another example of what I call timefulness. The Japanese symbol or ideogram that ma is expressed in is that of the sun between two gates. It is both physical and mental in application. It is the rhythm in poetry to accentuate the ethereal, in dance it is the tension in-between the steps, in music it is the silence that connects the notes, and in the bow, it is the intention of time and depth to show respect. While it refers to emptiness, it is full of an abundance of energy, or expansion of ourselves. According to 18th-century dramatist Chikamatsu Monzaemon, *ma* means, *"The truth is in-between.*

As well, much of our English language is rooted in words of domination and dehumanization. Architects and realtors are finally changing the words they use to identify what was once called a *master* bedroom, and I stopped complaining about a burnt dinner, using the expression I *slaved over* it. In the documentary film, *The Doctrine of Discovery, Unmasking the Domination Code* by Steven T. Newcomb, we find a breakdown of the word "civilization," which carries with it the genocidal principle to civilize those of a lesser race or religion by those of a superior one. That, as Steven puts it, "is the organic law of the United States," referring to the dehumanization to civilize, and the genocide of the original peoples.

If we are to think, write, speak, and behave in the direction of our own integrity, we must pay close attention to the power of our words and thoughts and the *ma*, the truth in-between them.

Imagine beginning with our inner dialogue; the conversation and stories we experience in our head. Personally, I find I offer myself a lot of unsolicited advice, which is really another expression for criticism. I scold myself when I am disappointed in my thoughts or actions, and I judge myself unmercifully on occasion. The most powerful and important liminal space is between our thoughts. What transpires in that space determines our health, relationships, view of the world, and manifests in how we show up and the words we use.

There's a lot of chatter these days about needing a new dictionary for this purpose. It's time to adjust our language to better articulate how our brains are expanding as a species. I have coined a few new words to add to this New Dictionary. My favorite is *timeful*. Maybe one day spell-check will accept it as a legit word. In *Conversations With God*, Neale Donald Walsch introduces us to a new way of looking at words like *care-full* and *grace-full*, so now I typically only use *thought-full* and *mind-full* to express what I am writing with the weight and full-ness of the words. Our words are communication-energy manifested so why not express ourselves with integrity? Plus, isn't *care-full* more lovely and meaning-full?

The skills we practice help us build muscle on the framework of our Odyssey. The more we practice and apply them with intention, coupled with an ironclad will, and honor the time we are taking, we can listen deeply to our invitation. Without understanding the power of Kairos time, we are not giving the stew a chance to cook and harmonize flavors. Let it sit on your tongue to ruminate. The more we practice, the more time we give ourselves to discover its nutrient-rich savory-ness that results in the tastiest life.

Three
Devastating Grace

*It is said that before
entering the sea
a river trembles with fear.*

*She looks back at the path she has traveled,
from the peaks of the mountains,
the long winding road crossing forests and villages.*

*And in front of her,
she sees an ocean so vast,
that to enter
there seems nothing more than to disappear forever.*

*But there is no other way.
The river cannot go back.*

*Nobody can go back.
To go back is impossible in existence.*

*The river needs to take the risk
of entering the ocean
because only then will fear disappear,
because that's where the river will know
it's not about disappearing into the ocean,
but of becoming the ocean.*

~Fear by Khalil Gibran

Then, I met Greg. It was 1976. We fell fast in love. We were 15 years old. He introduced me to pot, Led Zeppelin, and slow walks on fire trails. I can still smell the scent of his clothes. From that moment on, any chance at finding my own authentic identity was lost and forgotten, to be rediscovered a decade later. I had no sense of self, no confidence in my opinion, let alone control of my life, my personal passions, needs, or aspirations. Wrapped up in what looked good to others, muddled with fear, I dare not think of what made sense. I had none.

However, I had someone I could trust, someone who filled a deep void in me with his love and who called me his own. And I know he meant it. I believed he saved me and made me feel worthy and safe where I was of no value to anyone until then, reinforced by the abandonment and disdain by my sister, conditional acceptance from my mom, and the fear of my father that I came home to every day.

After nearly a year, during one of our now-regular breakups, I learned Greg had impregnated a 14-year-old who was sent away to a home for pregnant teens. The moment I heard the news, I had crossed the threshold into discovering boundaries. I reached the departure gate on my Odyssey. I was not going back, but I was not sure I was going forward either.

I was inconsolable, but some girlfriends tried, and took me to a movie and afterward, a diner. I sat down at a clean table, except for an opened but otherwise untouched box of Marlboro Red cigarettes sitting next to the condiments. I did not smoke, but as I wallowed in my sorrow, and my girlfriends talked among themselves, for some odd reason I pulled the cigarettes out of the box, one by one. About halfway through, I looked into the box and saw something out of place. At the bottom was a little piece of paper. I dumped out the rest of the cigarettes and pulled out what appeared to be a fortune from a fortune cookie. Its words would change the trajectory of my life. My fortune said, "Life is a tragedy for those who feel, and a comedy for those who think."

The cigarettes had been neatly packed, by no other means but the packing machine. I tried to put the cigarettes back, but you just can't beat a machine pack job. Every time I saw a friend smoking Marlboro Red, I'd insist they empty their box, never apologizing or explaining this insane request in my insistent urgency to find another fortune, as if I were seeking out a golden ticket. But I never did find another fortune. I recently searched online for this, or anything close, but nothing came up. Since then, I have no other choice but to accept and believe in the mythological and the mysterious and leave it at that.

That was the last day I cried over this "Big T"-trauma. What followed was transmuting my sorrow to hatred. In retrospect, I imagine my angels crossed their arms, shook their heads, muttered an "Oh, dear Lordy," while rolling their eyes. "I guess we are far from done with this one."

I was not aware of it at the time but buried somewhere in the layers of pain of betrayal, abandonment, and shock, I experienced what I was made of. What I did not know then was it was the first time I found my power. At the time, it bore no resemblance to that, however. Instead, I crumbled to the floor, where I would stay for much of the next decade. I was devastated. My heart was shattered. I had discovered my boundaries which meant I could not turn back. No left. No right. No future. I was alone, right in the middle of where I stood.

It's a liberating feeling having the choice laid out in front of you. There's no wondering if you did the right thing because you did not have a choice. It was you or your integrity. We are all wired with a line in the sand. Only it's not always clear where that line is until it's too late to avoid it. You meet your evolving self at the cost of more pain, with no guarantee everything is going to be okay.

At some point, she finds herself at a point of no return. She has accepted the reality that the world is not what it appears to be. She comes to her call to action and reckoning. The veil is lifted off the innocence and there's no more fooling around. She has suspected this for a while now, yet the fear of stepping into this new reality is painfully hard to imagine. It's time to put on her big girl panties even though they are uncomfortable. Her new britches are too big for her, and yet, she has no choice but to somehow grow into them. The threshold is now behind her and the deal is done.

As illustrated in bold letters on the Hero's Journey, this is where departure, crossing the line of no-return, is met with trials, tests, and encountering big monsters and alligators. It's good to know that, according to the Heroes' Journey, discovering our treasure or reward is followed by a return to a happy, better life ahead. We just never know how far or how long it will take to get there, so we might as well enjoy the treasure hunt.

A good Liminal Odyssey is just that. This is where the rubber meets the road. The muscle to strengthen is the one of awareness; awareness that we have arrived at that threshold and now it's time to stop and breathe and not take another step until we recognize we have choice.

The quote from a box of Marlboro cigarettes, "Life is a tragedy for those who feel and a comedy for those who think." can be seen as cringe-worthy, but it was what the doctor ordered. It got me out of my heart, giving it a rest, time to cool down, and familiarize me with using cognitive tools to see the proverbial light. We know we need a balance between the two: heart and mind. We have a rational thinking brain for our very survival and other household uses. If left only to my emotions, my freezer would be filled with ice cream and coffee cups replaced with wine glasses.

Rational brain and all, I still spent the next seven years searching for the safe place where I thought love lives. I was desperate to get that feeling back, return to a place of safety, to be defined by someone who thought me worthy of his love. I sat on the edge of the cliffs and prayed for someone to love me for who I was. I prayed hard, and for many years. Having since learned about the power of being very clear with what we are asking for when praying, I never really stopped to realize that I did not know who I was, so of course, the prayer could not yet be answered.

But one thing I did know for sure: I knew how love felt and I also knew that hate was a very real, but misguided emotion. I wished Greg harm. I wished him ill. My nickname for him to my friends was "shit-head" and to me, it was fitting. I would not know what forgiveness felt like until meeting Greg 30 years later as an invalid, strapped to a hospital bed in a convalescent home that reeked of urine.

It would be a long time of floundering, climbing ladders, and feeling around in the dark, with no flashlight, bumping into disappointments and foolish behavior, hoping to feel what I felt when I last felt safe and loved, when my heart fluttered, and I was adored and treasured. I did not know I had a choice in the matter. I did not yet know it was me I was waiting for.

My mentor and guide, Grandmother Ocean, was there all along. She gave and gave everything I asked for, but in the end, it was me I needed most, and she knew that. Perhaps that is why she took so long to deliver.

Rather than jumping off, I sat for countless sunsets with my feet dangling from a cliff, down the road from the home where I grew up. For hours I sat and watched the whales watch me. I'd wait with faith that another would breach, and they usually did. The pelicans and seagulls entertained me as I waited. They all seemed very sure of what they had to do, where they needed to be and what their purpose was. I longed for that sense of purpose, and to be loved unconditionally like Grandmother Ocean loved me. Beyond the tips of my toes was a universe of opportunity, of promise, of mystery, of life that I could only imagine. I did not think too hard about it because I simply knew. I trusted her and I loved her.

As I started working and making decent money, getting positive and authentic feedback and affirmations, consuming books and lectures on self-motivation, and coming into my self-worth—as if she hadn't given me enough—I changed up my prayer. Realizing more of who I was, I shifted my request with more clarity of what I was praying for. "All I want is someone to love and accept me *unconditionally.* This was my new fervent prayer and therefore my promise. I recited this as if it were my creed, my life's vision, and mission statement. If, while sitting on the beach I would ask her advice, now I was sitting on the edge proclaiming my wish. I promised Grandmother Ocean this was all my soul required to be free. And one day she delivered.

He appeared. At first, I thought it was too soon. I was only now coming into who I was loving to be. I resisted. But he did not appear as the others, and I could not take a chance not having him in my life, knowing he was the answer I was waiting for. He was easy, kind, funny, and he loved me unconditionally.

35 years later, his love is still unwavering. Now that She knew I was clear on what I wanted, my prayer was answered.

Over time, I have come to believe my husband's angels were sent on a mission to find me as well. The treasure map that was the fortune in the bottom of a box of Marlboros led me to him. To an unwavering fault, he lives the theory and common statement that "Love is All That Matters." Sometimes it irks me when I try to gripe. He is the sacred art of listening embodied and I have been listened into countless conditions of discovery and disclosure of who I am. He also sees life as a comedy. Go figure!

My life was now framed as an active and good wife, mother, and better soccer and basketball mom. I was ever-present and co-created a healthy and happy family. But I knew that there was unfinished business—something I had to reconcile. I didn't know exactly what, but knew it involved Greg, which made no sense because I was living a charmed life, with an otherwise perfect family.

Now that Facebook and Google searches had evolved, surely I could find him and just take a peek at his life, and better, show off mine. He was not showing up on social media or any radar, but I did find his younger brother. He informed me that Greg had suffered a series of strokes and had been hospitalized for nearly 19 years, bedridden in a nursing home in San Diego, about an hour south from me. No one really knew how much he understood, and while he was somewhat responsive, did not expect him to live much longer, as 19 years in this condition was stretching it. He said I should visit Greg.

I walked into the depressing, dark, and musty smell of a convalescent home to find a disfigured and questionably coherent shadow of a man. I searched his face for some resemblance to who I remembered him to be. His moves were spasmodic, and his arms and legs were buckled down to keep him safe in bed. Then a small voice in my head said, *Did you wish this to happen?* After all, prayers work. Of this, I was certain.

I asked Greg if he remembered me, and his response, ever-so-difficult to spit out was, "S-s-s-s-sorry." At first, I assumed he meant, "Sorry, no," but then I decided to accept his apology, and responded with, "You are forgiven." Immediately I felt the "thud" of a 30-pound weight drop from my shoulders that I hadn't even realized I was carrying. I could hear it hit the floor. In that moment I decided I would come back regularly to visit, knowing his grown kids and ex-wife had abandoned him, his mother and older brother had since died, and his younger brother lived too far away. Only his father came regularly. Maybe I could help rewire his brain. The irony of it all made me smile. I would write a book about this one day, "scorned teenager reconnects with invalid first love who did her wrong 30 years later and rewires him back to life." I drove home grateful I had come and was working out how I could return weekly. My self-serving ego was enjoying this.

Looking back, this big T-trauma had nothing to do with a teenage boy cheating on his girlfriend and shredding another girl's high school dreams, let alone her life, with me as a lucky bystander. The physical impact on me was minimal compared to that of this teenage mother, yet it hit as hard because of the lessons I had to learn. Ultimately, I was gifted an internal ride on the T train that set me on this path. Forgiveness is a strange phenomenon. I am not one to will forgiveness. At a deep level, I could not grasp its definition. I would later come to understand why. Logically, I understand its value and the consequences of carrying the affliction of the hard feelings. However, I had yet to find the mechanical key to unlock the forgives portal, but in that moment at Greg's bedside, I experienced it for the second time in my life.

The first time I saw the light of what I understood as forgiveness was when my father died. It was as if there was nothing to protect myself from any longer; nothing to feel vulnerable about. I was finally free from the weight of a burden I carried and did not have a clue or the insight to put down. When my dad died, every issue I had with him just evaporated, replaced with seeing him in the light of compassion for the hard life he was just trying his best to get through.

I was recently led to the realization that I was seeing forgiveness through victim consciousness and was grossly missing the reality of the gift I was given in the form of a hard lesson. I have misunderstood its meaning to be the same as reconciliation, as if, with the decision to forgive, I could resolve the impact of the experience. Yet, that experience was woven into my being, and its impact was a gold-plated blessing. I now choose to alchemize the experience with gratitude and be thankful to the one who brought me that experience.

If this were a movie plot, and I wrote this into the story of the Hero's Journey, this would be the part where, with shoulders back and chin up to the sky, the dark clouds part and a multi-beam ray of sunshine lights up my face, and a light gust of warm breeze lifts my long hair off my shoulders for just a moment to cool my neck. This scene would be labeled, "Treasure/Reward," a stage of the journey where we can exhale. Aladdin kisses his Princess or Cinderella makes it to the ball.

The reward was not that my dad was gone, but that I could clearly see who he was beneath his crusty exterior. It felt like a privilege. I can now understand how forgiveness works as the window to see through the external power to a soul who is just looking for a way out.

That day in the hospital with Greg, I also found more of myself, and all the sweet, furry forest animals came out of hiding and began to sing. However, we have seen enough of these movies to know what's coming next, especially since we know this movie is about 70 minutes long and we are only 40 minutes in. Yes, she loses a slipper and there is more adventure ahead with more lessons to learn and reckoning to weather.

Soon after that visit, I called Greg's brother to let him know I would be returning to see Greg. He told me Greg had since passed away. Did a weight drop from his shoulders, too? Did he finally get a chance to apologize, or better yet, be forgiven so he could finally leave this earthly plane in peace? I choose to believe it. My ego is now doing cartwheels.

I wonder if the weight I carried would have dropped off by itself otherwise. After all, I did not know it was there except for an uneasy tug. Good thing I followed the thread into the opening of the Liminal Odyssey.

If you follow your bliss, you put yourself on a kind of track that has been there all the while, waiting for you, and the life that you ought to be living is the one you are living. Wherever you are — if you are following your bliss, you are enjoying that refreshment, that life within you, all the time.

-Joseph Campbell

Forgiveness, Sacrifice and Bliss

If the soul's purpose is to be free, then forgiveness is the liberating key to shed the chains that bind it. When we experience a moment of liberation, we must sit with it in awe and respect, celebrate our self, and bow to those we once considered villains and enemies for showing us the light.

We have been practicing and listening, and because we realize that moment in the liminal space, we naturally proceed in the direction of the soul's goal. While we may not be conscious of how we got to the destination and hear the reality hit the floor with a "thud," like any muscle that is conditioned, it has memory and will respond in the way it has been trained through practice.

In the myth of the hero, including the biblical story of Jesus, we find the eerily similar storyline of the sacrifice followed by the understanding that from death comes life. It's the original understanding of our agrarian ancestors who knew that burying a seed, putting it to its death, would resurrect new life, theorized by some as the derivation of the culture of burying our dead.

In many stories, warriors and activists skipped happily to the chopping block because it meant eternal life for them as the hero. I don't know anyone who would choose to be beheaded, or a path of suffering, but the act of living through any level of trauma is a heroic one. We just don't give enough credit to those who are going through it, or on the other side. In the linear fashion of the Hero's Journey, resurrection is the final stage, yet I would argue it comes also at the third rite of passage, the point of no return. The old perception of what we accept is gone, buried with who we were and reborn to who we are in the now.

According to the author, thought leader and theorist Gary Zukav's Multisensory Human theory (which I expand upon later) this would be a sacred moment of reckoning. In this excerpt from *Seat of The Soul*, Gary writes, "Our deeper understanding leads us to another kind of power, a power that loves life in every form that it appears, a power that does not judge what it encounters, a power that perceives meaningfulness and purpose in the smallest details upon the Earth. This is authentic power. When we align our thoughts, emotions, and actions with the highest part of ourselves, we are filled with enthusiasm, purpose, and meaning. Life is rich and full. We have no thoughts of bitterness. We have no memory of fear. We are joyously and intimately engaged with our world. This is the experience of authentic power."

This affirms for me that our soul's desire is to be free from external power and return to a state of bliss. The physical form that is you and me may not choose the guillotine, but maybe our soul will, as an attempt for freedom. The lesson our age-old ancestors taught us is that from death comes life, and the only way to get closer to freedom is to learn a lesson to lose our head over and wake up with a new awareness. The light goes on, you still have a pulse, you've dodged a bullet. Hidden hands were guiding you, disguised as betrayal and heartbreak.

In this evolved state of awareness, we can see clearly the path that led us here, all the fortunes and gems along the way, and we find our self in a state of gratitude. Our sacrifice and its purpose are unfolding. The pain and suffering were not wasted because our soul is closer to freedom. Its path is now paved with new lessons of gold filling, just like the art form Kintsugi mentioned earlier. When those cracks and fault lines of our raw experience are alchemized, the vessel is not only stronger but also far more beautiful. Our heart will never go back to its original shape because it has expanded. Its natural growth is intended to make room for more gold to fill new gaps. The plaque that builds around our heart appears to be as solid as concrete, but that's only an illusion. It can also be a glass façade with a new tint to see the world in a different light; a UV protection film that was well-deserved, like a lifetime achievement award. Whether we accept the prize and honor ourself or choose the hard, crusty buildup is our choice alone. Plaque is a natural by-product and is there for your protection, but it is only external power.

What appears as heartbreak, a negative experience, or disappointment is nothing more than a contrasting shade so we can see bliss. It is there to remind us what darkness is so we can become intimate with the light, our soul's longing desire, and home to return to. If darkness feels like death, it's comforting to know that from death comes life.

As we experience more love, more awareness, more heartbreak, more disappointment, more achievements, and again, more love and more awareness, both the plaque and the external protective glass begin to erode leaving one with a knowing, an open and accessible heart, and joy is quick to follow. We are the alchemist in our own life and only we can turn that plaque into gold. And this is possible because we are in our authentic power as opposed to external power.

Now we have cellular memory of that feeling. It may just be a glimpse at first, but we will notice it more each time we recall that feeling. The more we remember, the more we re-member from our higher-self perspective. And we will attract more and more people who share that frequency.

The same is true for choosing suffering, complaining, or victimhood. Notice who hangs around us and enjoys and contributes to the Debbie Downer Club. Choose joy and we are contributing to our soul's freedom. Then, notice the ones we attract and who we choose to be around.

To feel the darkness, in the immortal words of my son-in-law, "Ya gotta feel all the feels." Like sand in the oyster shell, it's there to define and refine us to our essential luster. We have to be vulnerable and let nature do her thing or we may miss out on a life-sized pearl of wisdom.

This yogic wisdom reminds me that pain is an ally and necessary to build muscle. And what better muscle to build than the Joy muscle. A muscle is a series of tissues grouped into a coordinated system for greater efficiency. I want more joyful efficiency in my life so I am going to pump joy as often as I can. It's the muscle located between our tickle bone, what makes us happy, reminds us of a feeling of resiliency, moves us to dance or hug, and/or a feeling of being in the zone, and the bliss organ, from where the ultimate state of joy flows.

When this operating system is strengthened and engaged, coupled with being in a state of integrity, life streams in grace. "Row, row, row your boat, gently down the stream. Merrily, merrily, merrily, life is but a dream." When we realize we are in someone else's rowboat and flowing against our own current, we can use the Liminal Odyssey methods to drop into the space in-between and change direction toward our dream's harbor.

Henry David Thoreau said, "Go confidently in the direction of your dreams. Live the life you imagined." I am living the life I imagined with every prayer, including a few bonuses I could never have expected: my husband. He laughs at everything. He clowns around, has one corny line after another, and keeps me on my toes to be careful what I say, as it may have a punch line. Yes, it can be annoying, but for him, life's a comedy, and that's what I called into my life.

I have been admired for having a flat stomach. I do 200 sit-ups a day, but that's not why I have abs of steel. Stop right now and laugh. Notice the muscles you engage. That's right, 35+ years of daily laughing gets you in shape the easy and fun way. It's also a great workout for your vagus nerve, the real Joy muscle.

One evening, when I was very young, my parents were going out to dinner and my mother was upset with my father. She went to get dressed and proceeded to put on her mascara. To do that, she had to raise her eyebrows. Immediately, every weight dropped off her attitude and she felt lighter, no longer angry. She began to laugh. From that day on, whenever I was sad, I hear, "Lift your eyebrows." Try it now.

Creating a state of happiness may begin with a raised eyebrow or a thought but is fully reinforced through our nervous system. It's as if the engineer who planned our physical being developed this support mechanism because we are literally wired to be in a state of happiness and contentment as our primary default system.

Dr. James (Jim) Doty is a neurosurgeon at Stanford University, author of *Into the Magic Shop: A Neurosurgeon's Quest to Discover the Mysteries of the Brain and the Secrets of the Heart*, former chair of the Dalai Lama Foundation, the Founder and Director of the Center for Compassion and Altruism Research Education (CCARE) and my friend. For the last 14 years, he and his team have focused on the neuroscience of compassion, empathy, and altruism, and the positive effects of such behaviors.

As the founder of Compassionate California, I spent eight years in a deep dive into the study and practical application of compassionate action initiatives and community building, and I was fascinated by the brain and body on compassion. From Jim, I learned not only the biology of compassion but witnessed what it looks like in real-time. I have watched Jim break down emotionally on stage, in front of hundreds, even thousands of people while telling a touching story because he is compassion-in-action. He is also a lot of fun, sometimes silly, and an example of the reality that compassion is often a byproduct of "true" happiness. (A recent photo taken of Jim in a Care Bear costume holding hands with Richard Branson pretty much says it all.)

Understanding the vagus nerve presented a whole new world to me, aligning my mind, spirit, and body for the first time that really hit home.

The longest-running nerve in our body, the vagus nerve begins at the top of our spine and runs through every vital organ. It is connected to our parasympathetic system that releases oxytocin and other hormones that promote well-being and other pro-social behaviors. It controls functions that allow us to turn our head towards suffering, set our gaze with kindness, regulate our breathing and digestion, and influences our vocal cords. Ever been stressed and experienced shortness of breath, or upset and your voice trembles? Viva las vagus! And, because it is activated when we feel or witness empathy or compassion, it is often called the compassion nerve. It may also attribute to the "mascara-emotion-lift-trick"!

When my kids were in a funk, having a hard day, or were simply having human moments, and when "lift your eyebrows" did not quite do the job, I found the fastest way to lighten up their state (and regulate their nervous systems) was to empty our pantry or go to the market and donate food to the local food pantry. Don't take it from me. His Holiness the Dalai Lama said it best, "If you want others to be happy, practice compassion. If you want to be happy, practice compassion." Why wait to witness empathy and compassion from others to activate your compassion nerve? Be the proactive compassion and happiness you want to see in the world.

Compassion is a verb. In the world of compassion activism, its definition is, "The ability to identify the suffering in another and the willingness to take action to lessen or alleviate the pain." Intention and will are a collaborative and active presence here.

There is an industry built around this action word including the development of many major university departments and centers around the world since the establishment of CCARE, including the University of California San Diego that received a multi-million-dollar gift to study empathy and compassion to cultivate those qualities in physicians.

As Jim says, "When you care, everything becomes possible." He refers to this state of compassion as one of transcendence recognizing we are all one and are interdependent. It is this realization that creates feelings of contentment, connection, and meaning and a place where we can reach our true potential.

The Liminal Odyssey is the place to drop into, take the time to reflect, refine, remove the wheat from the chaff, and clear all that does not serve us. It's permission to be compassionate with our self as we take a sacred moment of reckoning. Remember that our body is wired for compassion. Knowing it is set up with an alert system to protect us and working on our behalf to experience bliss is a great start. Then we can more readily, "row, row, row our boat," and "go confidently in the direction of our dreams." That's compassionate action.

Four
The Mother (of All Nations) of Invention

Finding the hidden truths of the soul, within the dream of life is the grand adventure. Fortunately, the Creator gave us clues, Universal Laws and Truths, mapping systems, signs, symbols, spirit helpers, and shamanic practices to assist us in finding our way home to our Divine selves, and to the experience of Oneness with Creator.

~Kathrine Skaggs, Artist, Shaman, Healer, Sage

On the morning of September 11, 2001, I awoke to the same scene the whole world saw. It replayed again and again. A cacophony of theories of Middle Eastern terrorism dominated the news. *Was Israel involved? What is going on in foreign politics? What's our relationship to Israel? What if it is Israeli terrorists? Surely, as a Jew, I would pay the price. What do I do with my children that morning? Should they go to school? What is coming next?* All of these thoughts tangled in my mind within seconds of seeing the second plane hit the building that morning. Then I heard, *Gather Women.*

I am not sure I had ever experienced such a broadcast before, but this was as clear as day. It was not a tug or a mortal cry. These were firm marching orders. I did not know where the orders were coming from, but my immediate and primal response was, "Yes." I sat up tall in bed with starch raging through my veins, hailed a firm virtual salute, and moved in the direction of finding women to gather.

My two feet hit the ground, I took a breath and said to myself, *What did I just say yes to?* I had no idea where I was to find the women. I was raising two middle school kids and wrapped up in their lives. I was also the Director of Sales and Marketing for a major home builder. I had no real experience around women other than the mean girls in school, dysfunctional and inconsistent relationships with my sisters, my best friend from seventh grade Linda, and my sisters-in-law.

By mid-morning I learned we were attacked by Islamic terrorists. I did not know any Muslims. All I could think about was what were Muslim mothers doing with their children that day? What was going through their minds? What about the women of Islam?

Orange County, California, was not designed with multiculturalism in mind. Neighborhoods are pockets of cultural distinction, and the borders are clear. There is no real mass transit, and communities simply do not mix as a natural byproduct of urban development. Yet, my rabbi, Allen Krause (of blessed memory) happened to have been one of the county's original interfaith activists and trailblazers for this sort of work to explore and celebrate the margins of our diversity.

One day a few years earlier, I was volunteering at the temple office when he announced he was having lunch with his clergy friends. Barely looking up from my work, I acknowledged him and told him I would hold his calls. He stood there for a moment. He said, "We meet each month." Again, I smiled with a nod, "Have a nice lunch." He stood at the doorway. He hadn't yet made his point, as if he knew that this would somehow plant a seed in my heart that would change the direction of my life forever. He proceeded to grab the doorknob to leave, but went on to state, with a half-smile, that these clergy friends of his were of different faiths, and they call themselves, "Men of the Tablecloth." He then opened the door and left.

The image of leaders from diverse faiths sitting at a table as friends in their respective regalia and head coverings was as corny as you could get when describing Peace Among Nations. Yet it warmed a part of me that reminded me of something familiar, something important, and something I should pay attention to.

Weeks before 9/11, and growing more curious about Jewish women's spirituality, I floated the idea of convening a sisterhood of a different kind at our synagogue; one that was not interested in meeting to discuss raising funds to buy chairs for the social hall, but a group of women who could meet to share and explore who they were as spiritual beings. It could also be an important space to share how we relate to our faith at a deeper level and bond as women who share a spiritual heritage. What could other women teach me about ritual and reverence for the female aspects that I was seeking in a faith I knew so little about? It was suggested I write a proposal and present it at the next board meeting.

Although I had three older sisters, none of them spoke of the depth of being a woman, of the value of sisterhood or of grace. They were busy with their lives and I was separated by a generation. Being that my sisters were teenagers when I was coming out of diapers, I missed out on a sisterly bond and having women nurture me in a spiritually profound way, ask me questions, cheer for me, and share stories and memories with me. I was longing for that. Not knowing what I was embarking on or realizing this was another form of a call to action, I stepped over the threshold into virgin territory and charted my path into creating a sisterhood that I was seeking in my own life.

I would present my proposal and find my Sisters, distinguished by a capital S. I would name the group "Miriam's Circle," as it was Miriam, sister of Moses, who is known as the protector of life, sustainer of spirit, and who led the exodus towards the land of promise with a tambourine and directions to the well. That board meeting was scheduled for September 15, 2001. It was cancelled.

The Liminal Odyssey

Here I found myself at a liminal place. I was in-between two worlds and I had a plan that no longer fit the bill. There was an internal combustion, an activation, a new call to action to gather women. It was time to reassess, reconstruct and get wildly creative. No, this idea could not be for Jewish women alone, but open to all women of all nations, so I named her Sarah, known by all the monotheistic faiths as the Mother of All Nations, and planted her in my heart. Sarah is also known to represent the promise of new life and fruitful expansion of possibilities in what may appear to be a barren seed but bursts onto the scene when the time is right, as promised by God.

A mentor appeared months before in the form of Sacred Listening guru Kay Lindahl, who was also the interfaith leader who worked with Rabbi Krause and led the first interfaith organization in our county. My first meeting with that group happened to be their last, but the genie was out of the bottle and a new potent seed was in the ground. Kay inadvertently gave me permission with a model of what was possible, so when the moment happened, I had something to wrap my mind and arms around. My first invitation was sent to Kay. On the Hero's Journey, this was my call to action and assistance had already appeared.

Just like our country, I was at a place where life was clearly not the way it used to be, and I did not know what was coming next. This is the place to stop and remember who we are as our authentic self, and a time to dream and let what is important float to the surface. The aspect of our self that, although we may have suppressed, could be our soul's only chance to proclaim its purpose. This time is a gift.

In the case of 9/11, the crisis came at the same time as my personal need for something new was breaking through. I already had a creative idea to change things up. Being timeful in this liminal space showed me I had no choice but to go back home and dream, giving me the spiritual nutrients to show up fully when the time was ripe. In fact, my bold audacious plan was a pencil scratch compared to the masterpiece yet to come. Because of Kay I had a clue, but no idea that seed would grow into a forest filled with life-affirming adventure.

It was not long after September 11th I was invited to a meeting, held at the local mosque, and convened by my rabbi, a priest, and an imam, organized by the county's Human Relations Commission. A group of about 20 of us would meet as part of a focus group. We were one of 32 groups meeting weekly for four weeks around the county in what was called "The Living Room Dialogues." We were the only group revolving between three places of worship.

Eight 6-foot tables were arranged in one large rectangle. Women and men from three faiths sat together with a mediator from the commission to guide us with questions, then report back the level of tolerance in our community.

I happened to sit next to Ghada, a petite, fiery, impeccably dressed Lebanese woman with a thick accent and a passion and drive that startled me. She spoke about her hometown of Beirut. She talked about living through the Israeli and Lebanese conflicts, the destruction done to her city, how she played the piano to drown out the sounds of gunfire and air raids. Her loud and dramatic hand expressions spoke volumes, accentuating her statements as she spoke truth with raw emotion.

Karen, a middle-aged Christian woman who walked in with a cane and on the arm of her minister, spoke from her high perch of intellectualism with a Harvard flare and well-seated confidence. I was highly intimidated by her intelligence.

Abe, a Muslim man, spoke about his mother's dear friend in Lebanon, a Jewish woman who, when she was a young newlywed, taught her kosher cooking. She always spoke with a fondness, illustrating the delicate impermanence of hatred among religions. He was kind, soft-spoken, intelligent, and genuine.

Across the table sat two stunning women wearing hijabs, both members of the mosque. They were both engineers. I looked down through the big space in the middle of our table arrangement and noticed their shoes. I was blown away by their styles, fine fabrics of their clothes, their poise, their grace, and highly educated and wise views of the world. I realized then that I had no idea what the rest of the world was about and experienced my first moment of "woke" through the lens of my white privilege and sense that I had so much more to learn, as did the American educational system. In that one evening, I traveled to Iran, Lebanon, Palestine, and Turkey through the deeply wounded stories of these compassionate, kind people.

Coupled with my desire to deepen my spirituality and connection to my roots, this meeting provided me with fertile ground to nurture the seed that Rabbi Krause planted on his way to his luncheon with friends. No doubt these were the women I was supposed to gather. Sprouts began to emerge from that seed and my DNA began to rearrange.

Our next meeting was at the synagogue and our third meeting at the church. By this point, we had grown very comfortable with one another. We were expected to hold four meetings and complete our process, but it was here where Father Crist presented us with a plan. It was obvious we had all developed very strong bonds. We joked about our past two Living Room Dialogue meetings that became "parking lot dialogues," some of us not wanting the conversations to end.

We could complete our commitment to the Human Relations Commission and regroup under the name "Common Grounds," then go off and work together. That night we devised a plan to go to Mexico to build a home for an impoverished family through the local organization Corazon.

The idea was so exciting that we brought a film crew with us that produced a documentary called *On Common Grounds* that went on to win several international awards. Somehow, I scored a leading actress role and was given the honor to present the homeowner with the keys to her family's new home.

The group Common Grounds never formally continued, but Karen would become one of my dearest friends, who urged me toward the threshold into what would be the manifestation of the next stage of my journey, which was to get serious about starting a women's group.

In 1982 my chrysalis/pupa stage began. Twenty years later, I would start to feel internal shifts and sprouting wings. Despite my early life's trauma, I had been safely cocooned until now. I had no choice but to emerge with all the beautiful parts of myself and fly.

If this were a movie plot, the main character would be faced with the life-or-death choice to muster more courage than she knew she had and all the strength in her bones to break through, defeat the challenge and reach the mountain top.

The Mother (of All Nations) of Invention

The butterfly must do this herself. Now, with all her curves and fancy wings she heads up and out with all her might. No one can help her. If she doesn't garner and direct her will, she will die. And when she does make it to the leaf to dry her wings, she can rest knowing what she is made of and that she has arrived at her authentic self. From there she also serves the greater purpose to beautify the world.

An idea to gather women was as new to me as knowing what to do with them once we were in circle. After all, I had no experience of having such relationships with women, let alone suggesting I become a leader of them. I had no experience with my own sisters who never all get along at the same time. I also had the residual of early childhood lack of confidence around women.

My sisters invented triangulation of fragile relationships. I grew up in a culture of unkindness from the girls in school whom I believed. I did not know how it felt to have a nurturing, compassionate and caring group of women around me that was consistent, but I longed for it in my bones.

The bodacious idea I heard that morning months earlier was about to spring from my lips. Standing on the dusty street corner in Mexico, at the same time the men (and one woman) were hoisting the roof onto the top of the house we had just spent half the day building, I mustered the courage to ask three women if they would be interested in having our own conversation. Almost before I could complete my sentence, Abe's wife Nadia, who has since become another one of my dear friends said, "YES!" and the others were equally supportive.

About six weeks later, 12 women stepped over the threshold into my home. These women all said, "Yes" to my invitation. I may have been the lone nut that day in Mexico, but they were the First Followers and became the midwives that night to birthing S.A.R.A.H., The Spiritual And Religious Alliance for Hope.

We were 13 women creating a beautiful garden we hadn't begun to imagine but would sprout in ways new to all of us. Each of us spoke of the women we emulate and honor, either from our traditions, our upbringings or in stories. "Who are you?" is really what I was interested in knowing. You can tell a lot about a person when you know who they are inspired by and admire.

At one point, I found myself out-of-body, looking around the room. I was lifted off the ground, watching something magical unfold. I could feel the energy swirling and spiraling around this circle of women. There was an unseen surge that propelled itself, like a tornado picking us up and gently placing us back down. Were our hearts beating as one? Had our biological flows synched, unlocking a sacred passage to a new dimension? I did not know what it was at the time but later discovered that what was pulsing through my veins that night was oxytocin. And it is accurate to say it was flowing for every one of the women in that circle.

This stress hormone is released at a time of tension to regulate our nervous systems. It is also released when in a state of compassion and empathy and is considered the maternal bonding hormone because it was first researched in childbirth. It's known as the "tend and befriend" hormone. The bonding agent between us that night was as thick as putty. I looked across the room to my friend who seemed flush. She felt it too. Later she pulled me aside and said, "We need to call Oprah!"

In 2002, and with an archaic internet, unrecognizable compared to what we have today, I found nothing on women's interfaith organizations. Nothing even came close. I concluded that collectively we were a unicorn; rare, beautiful, and strong. Our natural highlights of the rainbow were dazzling. Nothing like us existed. The fairytale of a unicorn has all the magical powers of the imagination and heart-centered intention. When she appears, we know that peace is within reach.

I pulled my shoulders back, took a big breath, and jumped into building a website. Similar to a land-grab in the Wild West, this was the new wild frontier of the world wide web. I knew something important was happening that was so much bigger than us collectively. I also felt a shift inside of me. I could sense a stretch and feel my butterfly hips expanding.

In the early years, we all marveled at her, this force of nature. We looked at S.A.R.A.H. as our little one and fawned over her like she was a precious gift the goddesses had entrusted us with. "It feels as though God is blowing in our sails," was a common statement among us.

When asked how S.A.R.A.H. was started, my go-to remark is, "I opened my front door and got out of the way." And that is exactly what happened. As a natural leader with a propensity to control my environment and take up a lot of air in most rooms, this was a surprise to me. I knew there was a sacred center and I was not it. My role was to let Her lead. I had no idea back then what a sacred circle was, but it was there, and I knew it at a level that was meaningful, so it came naturally and comfortably.

We learned circle process along the way, and by necessity. The circle then showed us how to be with one another. The sacred center grew in substance and girth, not to mention lots of multicultural food, adopted customs, and ceremony. We were safe. We hosted close to 200 monthly in-home meetings, welcomed impressive guest speakers, went on outings together, produced countless community events including seven years of a massive weekend of community service that cross-pollinated our diverse faith communities to work shoulder-to-shoulder on various projects. We catalyzed a thousand people out to hundreds of projects around the county to focus on their common bond of the Beloved Community.

Candlelight vigils on the steps of the AME Church, Synagogue, Gurdwara, or whoever had experienced senseless crimes against them was what we could be counted on to show up for with prayers and candles in hand. We were invited to sit on university panels, speak at major events, and accepted a few awards along the way, including a global award we accepted in India.

Because we are women conforming to our highest and deepest value systems, we were actuating a nurturing foundation for trust, compassion, kindness, and Love (with a capital L). Because of that sacred space anchored by a sacred center, we had fewer personality issues than we could count on one hand, and with hundreds of Sisters over nearly 19 years, those are some bragging rights. This is more proof that a culture of care and caregiving not only works, it is also enduring and resilient.

The responsibility of how I proceeded next required some reckoning with who I was. Often the call to action is a subtle hint that is not so much about finding our way through a crisis as it is recognizing our personal responsibility and agency with humility and integrity to find a new solution to an old problem. While we are professing creative solutions through compassion, grace, and authentic power, we must live those values ourselves, and we hold one another accountable. Herein lies evidence of organizations that are sustainable and can last the test of time, or at least 19 years.

Without intentionally doing so, I crafted a safe, trusting, and treasured Sisterhood that I had longed for since entering Kindergarten. It's true: while we cannot choose our family, we can choose our Sisterhood. I was able to be vulnerable in these settings. I could be myself, and the self I wanted to see in others.

A byproduct of this environment is wild creativity. We can play together, come up with silly, outlandish ideas that became award-winning initiatives. Together we stretch the boundaries because we are not afraid of snapping or someone getting their panties in a twist and picking up their toys and going home. We have a safety net, an "ouch" policy, that anyone can activate. All conversation comes to a halt. At that moment, it is all-hands-on-deck, and we don't move forward until we are clean-and-clear through a process of reconciliation and sacred listening.

Once again, my angels placed a doozy on me, providing the opportunity so I could crawl my way out of this cocoon by the life force of my Sisterhood. They, whom I called into being with a simple, "Yes," would be my propellent, cheering section, supportive guides, allies, angels, and companions into the new frontier.

My angels also came in the form of the indigenous Grandmothers, thought leaders, and a tsunami of introductions and invitations from women taking Earth-quaking actions. Some were of notoriety, moving big levers to thrust society forward, but most of them quietly contributing to the enormous shift of planetary transformation that is clearly underway.

It's as if we are each a shard of metal flake and someone dropped an electromagnet in the middle of us. The forces pulling us together leave us no choice but to connect. The root of our unifying shared vision is to bring an end to a five to ten-thousand-year-old era of patriarchy through the balance of the divine feminine and the divine masculine. We have complementary or radically different methods to get there, but all share, through fierce or subtle advice, the value systems of collaboration, generosity, and hospitality. We also all have something to offer that supports another to accelerate their goals, which is always mutually beneficial. In the end, we are all better when we are all better prepared for what's to come. I believe the future is feminine and so does everyone in my tribe. This awareness is alive in the relationships I have near and far, and especially in the men who are discovering the freedom and magic of circle, which I touch on in chapter six.

In 2006, I was invited to a small focus group at Harvard University by Kathryn Lohre, then the Assistant Director of Harvard University's Pluralism Project, and hosted by its founder Dr. Diana Eck. We met to explore what was sensed as the next wave of feminism through the women's interfaith movement for their report, *Women's Interfaith Initiatives in the United States Post 9/11*. The days of pumping our fists and pounding the pavement were behind us. Now conforming to our higher and deepest belief systems appeared to be the fastest way to enduring and sustainable peace. It was Kathryn's warmth and calm, sensible presence that eased my nerves as the least formally educated person sitting in a room on a campus where possible every great mind has passed through for nearly 400 years.

Only three of the approximately 17 that were invited resembled grassroots women's community-building. The resemblance was more than remarkable. We referred to us as triplets separated at birth because of the phenomenon that we did not know about one another until then, yet all seemed curiously identical. No doubt that was another idea hurtling through space that, like a skipping stone on a calm lake, hit all of us the morning of 9/11. Indeed, we were three unicorns separated at birth. We went on to collaborate, share best practices and models, and we grew exponentially because of that meeting. That is feminine leadership. Collaboration, mutual-support, care and caregiving, interdependence and reciprocity are nature's way and we three were a mini eco-system.

The Liminal Odyssey is more than a playground of exploration, dreaming, and recreation of something old into something new and fantastic. It is largely a preparation process for the places we *can* go. And where we do go largely depends on how prepared and clear we are. This is where we get to question and turn assumptions on their side and look at the undercarriage. If we are sincere in having the most intention-filled journey, we are best served when we listen to our nature and the natural world around us. This is the source of our most potent messages if we open our inner and outer eyes.

Once, before time existed, an ancient Divine Mother-Grandmother Spider, also known as the Weaver of the Web of Life, sat quietly in the Sky World. She waited for the awakening of the Great Cosmic Womb, the place of all Creation.

As the Great Cosmic Womb began to awaken, Grandmother Spider took a very deep breath and began to sing a weaving song of energy, connecting the stars and the Spirit Doorway through which all life is birthed. Color, light, and song danced through the Universe, connecting all from the invisible to the visible world. The web gave birth, and the creative process was born, giving life and the specific vibrations of sound and color to the dream of each spirit being coming into form. As Grandmother Spider sang, she helped souls weave their own specific lessons and experiences with the Dream of the earth walk. Within the Web of Life, Grandmother Spider connects us all as One in Spirit.

Grandmother Spider- The Weaver of the Web of Life
A Hopi Story, as well as many other tribes of Southwestern North America
-Katherine Skaggs, From the book *Healer Shaman Sage: Timeless Wisdom, Practices, Ritual, and Ceremony to Transform Your Life and Awaken Your Soul.*

We Are Nature

Observant Jews pray five times a day, and there is also a prayer for just about every household act. Muslims also pray five times a day, in a very specific manner that is both orderly and expressed through a yoga-esque life force-generating flow of prana, the life force energy. There is also a melodic call to prayer called the *adhān*.

I am more of the prayerful type to run a constant prayer line, always in communication with Source/Great Spirit/God, in that I never put down the receiver.

However, meditation is more methodical and a discipline. For me, the practice of meditation is one of being the sacred listener. With exception of listening to my body suggesting it's time to check-in, convene with my breath and call in a few gurus and ancestors, I am more of a scheduled meditator. Especially twice a day when I have two calls to prayer. One is my pillow at night, and the other is the hoot of an owl or a morning dove, which wakes me from my slumber or trance on most mornings. When I was a little girl, it was often the foghorn on the cliffs below, usually followed by a chorus of seagulls.

My personal relationship with religious observance is the latter and I believe was the original intended call to prayer and to meditation. Both come with the condition of needing to wake up and listen to our natural world. The roosters, owls, seagulls know what to do, and we are well-served when we listen to their calling.

Several years ago, I hosted a webinar that welcomed Belinda Eriacho, a Diné and Aswii Elder, whose stunning statement was captured on the call recording. With permission, I am quoting her here:

> "The trees, plants, and grass that grow upon her are like her hair. The stones and rocks are like her bones. The water and natural resources that flow in her are like her blood. Until we know her as a living, breathing being, it's only then that we can honor her."

Elder Belinda was referring to honoring our Mother Earth. The relativity of the rhythmic dance between women and Mother Earth is remarkable. Women's biological imperative is to birth new life, sustain our environment, nourish our families and communities, protect us from harsh conditions, control the ecosystem of our world and work in collaboration and cooperation for the next seven generations. In a woman's wholeness is a rhythmic connection to all of nature, one that is as serious as a heartbeat.

It makes sense then that like the tree, we share a root system with our natural world. When we are not in accordance with our own nature, that which our own inner guidance is designed to lead us to, then our roots begin to die a slow death. Some deaths are slower than others, but because the roots are buried under the surface, usually deep, deep down, and laced around other roots, we only can rely on two indicators: 1) paying attention to our body signals, and 2) symbolism that something is calling us to a meditation practice.

A knot in the throat, back pain, clenched jaw, or sudden racing of the heart beckons our attention. A "gut feeling" is not an inconsequential feeling and is taken too passively if not truly honored for what it is saying. All are invitations to stop, drop down, and listen to that root system, which is always connected to a chakra center; the energy-processing center within each of us.

A high-level understanding of the chakra system is that it is our spiritual nervous system, illuminating the movement (or blockage) of prana; life force energy that can help us understand ourselves. The vagus nerve is the communication devise alerting the bells to ring. Just knowing the throat chakra is related to my communication energy, when I feel a trembling or a knot in my throat, I know there's a block and it's calling my attention. I can explore the fear of speaking up, the sense that my words are not being heard or honored, or I am not speaking in my integrity.

Each chakra is associated with a color, element, musical note/tone, statements, and many more expressions. Gems and crystals are used to clear or harmonize specific chakras, and the ancient origins and practices to align the chakras is an education worth accumulating. There are seemingly endless resources of books, courses, and videos on better understanding the chakra system.

Like the trunk of a tree, the root chakra is located at the base of the spine, the pelvic floor, and is responsible for our sense of safety and security. Strong roots ensure a solid foundation for the balance of energy flow throughout our body and our life. When our bodies feel threat, sorrow, shame, regret, or longing, we need to stop and pay it the respect it deserves. It is never wrong. It's trying to tell us something. Regardless, listen as if our body was nature itself, because it is.

The symbols found in nature, including our natural self, are billboards for information, and medicine recommended for daily use. As an example, the symbols and synchronicities of hearts in my life are significant. I married a Hart, who makes sure any jewelry he brings me is in the appropriate shape. Heart gifts coming to me are heart-warming. A heart is an icon I can sign with my name, and often do. However, these hearts are manmade expressions of love we can all relate to. We are lucky to have such a symbol in our culture.

Readily finding heart-shaped clouds, heart-shaped cracks in the cement, spots on animals, and knots in trees mean we are able to see the love in the natural world. You'd be hard-pressed though to find a naturally heart-shaped desk in a boardroom. Heart-shaped leaves, rocks, and a rare find in a piece of fruit or nut are random gifts of nature that make finding them all the more awe-inspiring.

While writing this chapter, my eyes caught something moving on the floor. I caught the last moments before it slithered under my side table. It looked like the last two inches of a mouse tail that had picked up some lint, but not exactly. Since I am not afraid of such critters, especially ones with interesting tails and being curious who was in my room, I picked up the table and there was a centipede. I grabbed a card next to me and slid it under this little fellow. Holding the card with care, I rushed it to the front door and set him free in his more appropriate environment. Then I sat down on my bed to inquire about the symbolism of a centipede appearing now. It must be decades since I have seen such a creature. Why, as I am writing about synchronicity and symbols of nature, and happen to also be reading a book and tarot cards on spirit animals, would this little guy appear and what might I make of it? Why was it calling my intention? What does it mean?

As synchronistic affairs can go, the card that became my little houseguest's shuttle to freedom was one of the Katherine Skaggs' collection of Spirit Animal Tarot cards, which I had not yet spent a lot of time with. Just gifted these cards by Katherine herself, they were sitting on my bed because I was sent on a mission from my friend Maureen, who knew I was experiencing physical ailments.

Because I really do practice what I preach, I set out to see where the disconnect was, and which root needed untangling. Maureen, who introduced me to Katherine, invited me to find my totem animal and "work with it." While Katherine provides light instruction on how to "work with it," largely she leaves it up to us to find our own way. Slowly I went through the deck and stopped at the Phoenix Rising card. Something came over me. I had felt this feeling before. I then immediately drew a new line in the Indra's Net of my life and Maureen was the pearl of connection.

In 2018 I was at The Parliament of The World's Religions in Toronto and invited to address a room of 400 high school students. As I headed to the conference hall, a friend stopped me to tell me he had just heard that morning about the birth of a white buffalo calf in North Dakota. This was also in the height of the Dakota Pipeline crisis which added significance to the already powerful message of this birth. It is prophesized that the birth of a white buffalo is a sign that peace is on the horizon. It is not unusual that tribal leaders from around the world attend this international event, but this particular Parliament was said to have been extremely important to the global community of indigenous peoples. I had heard from the leader of the Indigenous Task Force for the Parliament that some medicine tribes were coming off their ancestral land for the first time in their history because they had something important to tell us. It was time for them to step out of their cultural ways of prayerful activism in a collective, louder voice. The timing of the birth of this calf was significant and created a buzz in the hallways.

The speakers before me presenting to the crowd of well-behaved students were three indigenous women elders. As they stood at the top of the room, I noticed something. They had come to impart important indigenous wisdom and sing and drum. From where I stood, it appeared the drum had a white buffalo calf painted on it. *Wild synchronicity worth noting*, I thought. I was amazed but went on listening to their message. Then, as they began to drum, I was caught up in its grip. Suddenly I found myself swept up and outside of my body. As if I had a hollow rod running down my spine, my back was erect with my chin up. I felt weightless, and there was an unobstructed energy flow from my womb to the crown of my head. I was standing in a fire but the energy flowing through me was cool. When I picked up the Phoenix Rising card, examined the art, and began to think about why it resonated in me, I felt the exact same cooling sensation. I did not recall it. It recalled me. I guess I found my spirit animal. Or more accurately, it found me.

Immediately after completing my first draft of this chapter, while sitting on my beach chair with sand in between my toes and the waves cheering me on, my gaze moved from my laptop to the water. Out of the corner of my eye, I noticed a large stone, half-buried but peeking out of the sand. It was not a rocky beach, so this seemed out of place. I felt the call to dig it out. It was just your typical odd-shaped rock. But underneath it was another, so I pulled it out, unveiling it slowly because, once again, I had felt this feeling before. I knew what I would unearth before it was completely revealed. I excavated a nearly perfect heart-shaped stone. It's more than symmetrical. It is concaved in a way as to hug my soul. I learned a long time ago not to take a natural item from its resting place without asking permission. I asked and She answered. She said I could keep it. In fact, I sensed she left it buried for me, knowing I would have the faith to seek it out.

The beach was getting crowded around me, so I packed up and dragged my chair about 20 yards away. I sat down and noticed, in almost the exact same angle from my chair as my last discovery, another rock peeking out of the sand. I knew exactly what it was. Slowly I pulled it out to uncover another heart-shaped rock, the same size and almost as perfectly symmetrical as the first. However, this one tapered to a thickness at its point. Its meaning intended to take me into a deeper place, and I will continue to explore that point. For now, I knew this was my reward for paying attention.

Sometimes it comes in an "aha." Sometimes you can hold it in your hand and feel its energy, a talisman to carry or place on a shelf or altar to remind you of your sacred nature.

In my beach bag that day was Katherine's book *Artist Healer Shaman Sage, Timeless Wisdom, Practices, Ritual, and Ceremony to Transform Your Life and Awaken Your Soul*. Each chapter begins with a full-page image of the Spirit Animal relating to that chapter (which Katherine painted in the most sacred manner, like the cover of this book). I also had a card, the same animal totem that dons the front cover of her book, the same size as the page. I was using it as a bookmark. When I picked up the book, the card fell out and I tucked it between the pages for safekeeping. Later I came to the page where I randomly tucked in the card and noticed it facing me. On the opposite page was that same totem animal! Two full pages of Jaguar Shaman staring back at me got my attention. I turned the card over to read the description that Katherine care-fully includes for all her cards.

"Jaguar Shaman Medicine for Awakening the Mind and Illuminating the Soul
Intention, Realization, Shape Shifter

Jaguar Shaman comes to you with the power to connect your inner consciousness with the creation of your outer reality. Jaguar is the totem energy needed to help you activate your Awakened Mind. The Jaguar Shaman is here to help you work with the power of intention to create and share shift your reality.

The Jaguar Shaman is a master seer, seeing the workings of Spirit in all of the physical world. She will help you align with your highest Self, impregnating your physical reality with love, wisdom, and the power of light.

This powerful Jaguar Shaman connects you to the vastness of Creation and all potential that exists beyond the limitation of your 3D self. Take time to focus and look beyond all distortion. Observe within and without. Love is the only path. Open to your intentions that align with your heart and soul passions. This will shape shift your entire existence. If this image has inspired you today, notice how you feel, and ask for your clear, soulful, heart-centered intentions to arise fully in your awareness, fueling your life into form. You are the awakened share shifter and creator of all you dream and experience."

Continuing on this particular joyride on my Liminal Odyssey, I picked up a reward of discovering this book's Spirit Animal, the Jaguar Shaman, and my latest ally in the form of a centipede.

These signs and symbols are essential elements on the Liminal Odyssey. They are definitive signs and calls-to-action. Applying the same process of listening our soul into a condition of discovery and disclosure of what is happening inside, acknowledging our allies, drawing the line in the Earth with intention and a will that has abs of steel, and excavating clues with our higher self, leads to whole-body contentment and health.

Five
Timeful Re-union

Synchronicities and coincidences are the vibrational matches of your soul's calling, manifesting in form.

~Katherine Skaggs

I had not given the Peace Sunday incident much thought since selling the car with the homemade bumper sticker on it that said, "What About The Dog?... Peace Sunday."

Nearly 30 years later, my friend Ruth and I drove together from Los Angeles to Northern California for an interfaith leadership summit. I share more about Ruth later, but for now, it's important to know she considers herself an "interfaith junkie," so "activist, author, composer, and key-note speaker" are understatements.

After our first evening meal together, we were invited to gather around the oversize stone hearth that looked like it was modeled after Gaston's lodge fireplace in *Beauty and The Beast*. Our convener Rev. Paul Eppinger stood up and suggested we all share one interesting story about ourselves. I went blank. I had nothing. I hadn't done anything remarkable and certainly not "interesting."

Nonetheless, I courageously walked up and took my place, front and center facing a small half-circle of lovely people, mostly strangers, not having a clue what to share, and out of my mouth came, "What about the dog?"

I told that story with trepidation, having never shared it with anyone in this manner, and about 20 years after the event. It felt like a cute little human-interest story at best. As I told the story, I found myself surprised at its wonder, and everyone else seemed to enjoy it too. I sat down with a passing amazement and did not give it another thought until about a year later when Ruth and I would find ourselves in Arizona at another interfaith conference, part of The North America Interfaith Network that gathers about 100+ interfaith leaders from around the country and moves from state to state, host to host.

This year it happened to be hosted by none other than the Rev. Paul Eppinger and his interfaith organization and community. Each year, the conference, which lasts a few days, always closes with a banquet. I could not stay for the banquet, needing to get home to my family. Not much longer after getting home and dropping my bags my phone rang. It was Ruth. She said, "'Sande, the banquet just ended, and I had to call you. Tonight, at the banquet Paul stood up to make his address and told a story. He started by saying he did not recall exactly where he heard this story, "but it goes like this." Then Paul proceeded to tell your story about the dog!'" Ruth added, "When he was done with the story, I stood up and shouted, **"That was Sande Hart!"** Ruth went on to tell me that immediately Betsy, who was also with us in Northern California, then stood up from across the banquet hall and said, **"And the dog is fine!"** That was the moment I realized I probably should start paying attention to the value of this story, and the stars began to head into their formation.

About a year later, I was invited to speak on a panel with the late, great Leland Stewart who, if there was an original interfaith activist, Leland was the man. He was a legend for us interfaith "junkies." I was thrilled and honored to present with him. Leland lived about 40 miles north of me at the time. He was elderly and not comfortable driving, so when I was contacted by a mutual friend asking if I would drive him, I jumped at the invitation. The idea of holding Leland captive in my car to glean all his wisdom excited me. As soon as he got in my car, I started in with my inquisition. I wanted to learn as much as I could from him. He was a kind and soft-spoken man, and humble beyond his experiences and wisdom.

He and his wife founded the International Cooperation Festival in 1965, which was during the United Nations International Cooperation Year Festival of Faiths gathering of 2,000 interfaith folks. It was the largest event of its kind, short of the first Parliament of World's Religions in Chicago at the World's Fair in 1893. He was quite proud and told me he and his organization had planned the next event in 1982 at the Rose Bowl and called it *Peace Sunday*. He proceeded to say, "...but a music producer took it over and it turned into a big no nukes rally and rock concert." He was clearly disgruntled as he waved his hand to dismiss the value of it all, as if to say, *those long-hair rock and roll hippies had sabotaged his noble plan*. I almost pulled over to the side of the freeway just to process the remarkable odds and serendipity of it all.

I shared with Leland my experience of how that hippie affair impacted me (and the dog). I am not sure he grasped the gravity of what it meant for me to be in this moment with him, but I can remember the sound of his giggle when I told him. I was hoping he would accept my story as evidence that all was not lost with his original plan and perhaps, in my small way, will live on to improve some lives. In that way, telling (and retelling) the story feels like a mission of its own. Each time I tell or write about it, I tip my hat to Leland and his journey that brought me that opportunity, ever so indirectly. Following the threads and connection points is essential on the Liminal Odyssey.

In the moment just before his giggle, a shift happened inside my world. This medium-sized synchronicity was now of epic proportions. The stars and heavens that began their formation one year earlier had completed their alignment into a magnificent constellation. Now I could see an invisible thread and a story coming into focus. This shot me into an Odyssey if there ever was one. I just could not fully recognize or name it until I was well into writing (and rewriting) this book.

Over the years, I tried writing that story. I was urged to, especially by Ruth, but it never seemed quite right, so I kept putting it down. In retrospect, I had more living and growing to do, and deep down I knew its time would come in the right way with the right muscle strength that could only be acquired by the following 10+ years of education, allies, teachers, mistakes, trials, heartbreaks, and joys that created the perfect condition for when that meteor would hit my forehead.

When I came to see threads of multitudes of different sizes, colors, and densities connecting in a sacred manner, the Liminal Odyssey was writing itself in my life. In that moment, sitting next to Leland, I became acutely aware of the meaningful spaces in-between in Kairos time.

Leland is the author of the voluminous book, *World Scriptures*, which he compiled and edited in cooperation with the respective communities represented. After graduating with a master's degree in mathematics, he was heading to Harvard Business School when an encounter with a man in a library challenged his Christian beliefs, leaving him spiraling up into a newly discovered spirituality. He changed his major that day and was accepted into Harvard's School of Divinity, which he graduated from in 1953. So, by all accounts, he was an expert on world religions and a spiritually inclined man. From my experience over the nearly two decades that followed until his passing, and as a friend, he was much more. He was "entire," as I have learned from his book on the Taoist philosophy on humility, "Be humble and you will remain entire."

Clearly, Leland's journey included an ally who was a stranger in a library. That ally was apparently mine as well.

When gifted with moments of clarity, we too can slide into the liminal space, a spacious room, as between the letters and the lines, to investigate, explore, maybe move around the furniture to see what's hidden under the sofa, what clues make sense now and what mysteries may be solved or maybe even realize (with real-eyes) we are on our Journey.

I could see clearly more wizardry of Kay Lindahl, the mutual friend who recommended I give Leland a lift that day. She must have been listening.

You'll See It When You Believe It:
The Way to Your Personal Transformation
Title of a book by Wayne Dyer

Sacred Cultivating of Synchronicities

Somewhere I heard the quote, "That which you do not believe you cannot see," but cannot find the author or quote anywhere. Perhaps it was my summation of the title of Wayne Dyer's book, but it is something I remind myself of and have regurgitated countless times, especially when I think or hear, "That's unbelievable!" or "You are not going to believe this." If we are to take the gift of experiencing synchronicities seriously, we ought best to believe it when we see it because we couldn't if we didn't. Mind twists are fun.

When one or more "signs" appear that are too related and meaningful to ignore, the tendency is to immediately think *What does this mean?* It's a common response while standing in the liminal space when slowing down for inner reflection, exploration, and looking deeper at the message. It's a pause because something new is coming through; a new understanding of our self and the world. The moment we start seeing meaningful connections, and the truth that has been waiting to break out of the subconscious trance, is the moment we enter the Liminal Odyssey. Since we cannot un-hear these messages and unsee the signs, we are at the point of no return on the Hero's Journey.

The more we notice them, the more they appear because we are paying attention and reprogramming our brain to tap into those possibilities. When we get to the meaningful part of the connection, they are often surprising, delightful, and full of joy and wonderment. Adding to the delight is the otherwise "mundane" event in which it typically appears. Acknowledging the gift with a nod, a round of applause, a bow, or a simple, "Aha" helps us embody the experience. I have shouted with glee several times in my life, and a few times while writing this book.

As I was thinking about this particular chapter, I had a coinciding of six synchronistic gifts.

I had been struggling with a relationship and, without realizing it, playing the blame game. Then, I heard a joke. It goes like this: A man went to his doctor and said, "Doctor, my entire body hurts. When I touch my head, it hurts. When I touch my arm, it hurts. When I touch my leg, stomach, and chest, they hurt." The doctor ran some tests, then came back to the man and said, "Well, the good news is, there is nothing at all the matter with you. The bad news is your finger's broken."

Aha! I was blaming my personal pain on everything but it's broken perspective. Within minutes of hearing this joke, this quote appeared on my news feed on social media:

> "When you blame and complain, you are admitting publicly that you are not wise enough to find the answer to your own problems." ~ Rev. Michael Beckwith

This gave me a big smile and a pregnant pause to honor the gifts laid out for me in bright colors (and a reminder of why social media can be good) then reframe my perspective and see my role alone in my situation, looking at my "broken finger" and grinning at the three fingers pointing back at me. Within an hour, I received an email from my best friend with whom I have been sharing parts of my book and who has subsequentially been having her own hosts of experiences-turned-experiments, which is why she was compelled to send me this text, referring to the intuitive that she visited.

"...[She] told me that a female relative who wears a yellow dress is close to me and will let me know they are around me by finding pennies. A week later I pulled into a parking lot, got out of my car and there were like 30 pennies right where I parked. So I am so grateful to find pennies. They make me smile.

Now Linda's radar was fired up and she recalled, "About a month before I got laid off from the horrible job, I found a dime and a penny in the work parking lot. I thought that was odd. But went on my merry way. Three days later and in a different parking spot, I find a dime and a penny. I kept finding 11¢ in different parking lots. It is not like I am searching to find money. But there it is …a dime and a penny. After I was laid off, it seemed everywhere I went I would find 11¢. I have a drawer with pennies and dimes. Realizing this brought me comfort during an uncertain time that someone was communicating, letting me know I am not alone. I got this, and good things will come. Life will change."

When I wrote her back, I told her I was wearing a yellow dress as I was reading her email. It was a stretch, but worth sharing. We never know where those little connections may lead. More importantly, acknowledging even the slightest of coincidences strengthens the muscle of awareness.

Two days later, Linda sent me a photo of the palm of her hand with two dimes and two pennies that she found together. She sent subsequent texts or emails like, "Found 11¢ by my bedside this AM." I wondered if these signs were synchronistically-ordained, or was it our conscious mind seeing what we needed and wanted to show us? It was both.

The next morning, my Daily Horoscope app said, "You may be telling yourself that a series of signs or serendipitous events is nothing more than a coincidence. It must be, right? You have a scientific mind Aquarius, and you know that there is a simple explanation for everything. But don't allow that kind of logic to be your enemy today or to hide a higher truth. As an intelligent person, you also know that sometimes the universe does offer us signs, and that may be what you are experiencing right now. If you can see it that way, those signs can lead you down the right path and give hope." Ya think?

During this same period, while sitting on the beach, a flock of pelicans, my favorite birds, flew overhead. For some reason, I counted them. I have never done that before, but because of Linda's story, I gave it a shot. I counted 11. I snapped a photo and sent it to Linda.

These words were written just feet away from where my toes once dangled off a cliff as a teenager. The surroundings behind me have been transformed since then from empty fields into a manicured park with a small museum, walking paths and benches, markers to count the whales, a small amphitheater, and resting places to inspire moments of awe and wonder. In front of me, however, the scene remains unchanged. The soft approach of the waves from as far as the place where the sun sets seem to be coming to greet an old friend. The smells, breeze, and sounds prove timeless, as if I never left. This place is home for my soul.

Then, another formation of pelicans flew overhead. Now that I am paying attention and questioning if pelicans only fly in flocks of 11, I count them. This time there were 14. Then 9. A little later, and almost immediately after having a typical hearty dialogue with Grandmother that came with clarity and resolution to a problem I had been facing, another flock came. This time they flew uncharacteristically low and close to me. As if to affirm this clarity, I counted 11.

We never know how our stories and our lives will impact others and invite new synchronistic experiences. How else would that confirmation of 11 pelicans have been noticed had Linda not shared her story and I not listened with intention? While so many have made my Liminal Odyssey extra-ordinary, I have to expect I may be that for others, too. I see this as a responsibility of humility, vulnerability, and being impeccable with my thoughts, actions, and words. As long as I am not the villain or monster in anyone's journey, I can say I succeeded.

Several years ago, I joined a group of interfaith leaders representing Southern California to attend the Carpe Diem Multicultural Conference in Guadalajara, Mexico. We joined others like us, primarily from Central and South America, and we met in a 17th century building that was once a military headquarters, but it looked like a 300-year-old monastery. It was a beautiful brick building with three stories overlooking a large courtyard that had no ceiling other than the heavens. It was a perfect setting in the center of a quaint Mexican town.

400 chairs were set up in rows in the courtyard with an aisle down the middle for the opening ceremony. One by one, tribes from South, Central, and North America filed in, one after the other. Each came bearing bowls of fruit as offerings. There were drums and rattles. Some were singing, blowing conch shells, or waving burning sage. Some were solemn. Some were dancing. Two little boys with drums flanked the stage in their loincloths and anklets and arm amulets of vines. With faces painted like their older tribal members, they were just a foot taller than the drums they were beating with an intensity of their heritage and community. They called in the ancestors along with the

men who were also drumming feverishly. Men and women proceeded down the aisle in their traditional tribal ceremonial dress, some with 6-foot-tall feather headdresses, shelled anklets, and a kaleidoscope of colorful regalia that varied dramatically from one tribe to the next. Some women were dancing and twirling and actively swirling up the energy in the courtyard.

The more tribal members that came, the more profound the energy could be felt, as if caught in a cyclone. I was catapulted into the current as their beads and shells got louder and louder and their feet moved faster and faster in tighter and tighter circles. The temporary tarps covering the open courtyard were struggling about more actively by the wind outside that seemed to pick up velocity. This went on for 40 or more minutes. Suddenly, we heard a huge gust as the tarps were blown off and it began to rain. This did not strike me as unusual because it was quite warm and about 90% humidity. We all retreated to the covered four borders of the courtyard. I had heard of rain dances working and I knew this was one of those times. But then, it began to hail, hitting the courtyard floor and empty chairs with unapologetic power. The hail eventually stopped, and the ceremony continued.

When I began learning about synchronicity, I found myself experiencing such wildly unusual and rather magical and mystical moments that did not necessarily come in the form of meaningfully connected events or signs. The common denominator is being willing to witness the mystery of the universe without reason, only with awe and wonder about its lesson.

I had just witnessed human beings manifest a hailstorm and alchemize 98% humidity on a balmy Guadalajara night. I experienced the power of humanity, clear with purpose, in full integrity, and a consistency rooted in a culture of reverence for something greater than thyself. In the native people's way, that comes from the Earth, cosmos, the spirits, and the ancestors. For me, it resembled the same power of humanity, clear with purpose, in full integrity and consistency, on a hot summer day at an outdoor music festival no nukes rally. I started seeing and feeling something unique, and that which I later came to understand as the Tao, the oneness of the universe. I could see it because I believed it.

Setting the intention to see more synchronicities makes it not only possible but evident that we will have more and more mystical and magical experiences.

Then we can wonder more into the spaces in-between to see the meaningful connections for a predestined trip on a Liminal Odyssey.

*This is the first, the wildest and the wisest thing I know:
that the soul exists and is built entirely out of attentiveness.*

-Mary Oliver

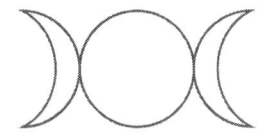

Six
Sacred Enoughness and The Red Tent

I wonder what secrets they hold?

~My 5-year-old neighbor, Maya Dotson,
while gazing at our local sacred mountains

While on a call with the Executive Director of The Goi Peace Foundation, I shared that I had written a report on Mt. Fuji in 5th grade and have always felt an affinity to the mountain in Japan. It was a passing comment after being asked if I had ever been there. Having no expectations to be sitting at Her hem several months later, I now recognize the glistening pearl of this connection point. Within a few weeks of that call, I received an invitation to participate in the Symphony of Peace Prayers event and symposium in Japan. As usual, I said, "Yes."

Gary Zukav is someone Oprah and I consider to be one of the single most spiritually prolific thought leaders of our time. I had the honor of spending a week in Japan with Gary, his partner Linda Frances, and about 20 other guests of Masami and Hiroo Saionji.

Masami Saionji is the chairperson of three world peace organizations: Byakko Shinko Kai, The World Peace Prayer Society, and the Goi Peace Foundation. She continues the work of her adoptive father, Masahisa Goi, who initiated a movement for world peace through the universal prayer *May Peace Prevail on Earth*. Every peace pole you see with that statement on it, usually planted in front of institutions, in parks, college campuses, places of worship, or in the background of any of my webinar videos is because of the work of Masami Saionji and her family. I think of them as acupuncture needles that attune world peace all over the planet, and they do.

Masami Saionji says, "Now is the time for each individual to recognize their own original power, the power of the inner sacred consciousness, which I call the Divine Spark." This quote reminds us of our personal responsibility to use our power of choice and recognize our inner authentic power; our divine spark to unlock and transform our consciousness for the emerging world of harmony, and one that works for everyone. (I have intentionally underscored the word responsibility.)

Our trip included a ride on the bullet train to Mt. Fuji and the Fuji Sanctuary, also founded by the Saionji's. At the base of this beautiful, and strikingly smaller-than-I-imagined mountain, I remembered what Maya said and could almost see Her Majesty's wisdom. She held secrets. And one was that I would come to Her one day for an important lesson.

We gathered on the first floor of the Fuji Sanctuary at the base of Mt. Fuji. There we sat on a room-sized handwritten mandala. Its pattern was created with the repetitive handwritten sentence, "May Peace Prevail on Earth." What seemed like hundreds of such mandalas were rolled up like carpet scrolls and stacked around this giant room. Each scroll, a mandala with the same repetitive sentence was dedicated to a different country of the world.

Gary spoke about "multisensory perception," which is perception beyond the five senses. In his book The Seat of The Soul that launched his record-breaking appearance score on Oprah, Gary writes, "Our five senses, together, form a single sensory system that is designed to perceive physical reality." The perceptions of what he terms as *The Multisensory Human* extend beyond physical reality to the larger dynamical systems of which our physical reality is a part. Further, he teaches that multisensory perception isn't multisensory perception until we recognize it and we use it, and I add, with intention and practice. When Gary spoke, I recalled in my body a feeling I could not name but shook me to my core. With reverence, I now understand what it was.

The results came in late the evening of the 2016 U.S. Presidential election. There I sat, straight up in bed with my back to my headboard and hands holding my womb as if I was protecting my next seven generations with my life. Every cell in my body was terrified and shocked. It was not a cognitive response. My psyche was stunned with paralyzing fear. I literally could not lay down and remained sitting up in bed for about two hours. Logically, I tried to reason that my gal did not win and, oh well. It would not be the first race my team lost. But this was something far greater than my five senses could recognize.

While sitting there frozen, a cellular memory jog was in progress; one catalyzed by a recipe of the senses I did not recognize because I had not yet read Gary's book and I was only relying on the five obvious senses I did know. All 37 trillion cells in my body were preparing for flight as if they had better run because the Nazis are coming. According to their memory, the sirens were blaring so they started to pack. I stopped them at the door with a new plan, with hands on hips, shoulders back, low resister in my voice, proclaiming, "Mother's got this."

It did not take long before the Million Woman March was organized and S.A.R.A.H. signed up to organize some women and attend. We also secured an exhibit table. But we would not just host a table and hand out disposable pamphlets. We had a better plan. It was the same impulse to gather women after 9/11 in my living room that prompted the idea to gather women into a Red Tent; a womb-space in the midst of this highly dynamic and energized flow of a reported one million people in the streets of downtown Los Angeles. If we were serious about standing up and marching together, we would need a safe and warm place to sit or lie down together in circle and go within the depths of our womanhood. After all, we are the majority vote and make up 80+% of all household buying decisions. A red tent is like a charging station for our power so we could step out fueled up and best prepared to heal our world. We also know, consciously or subconsciously, beyond the siloed five senses, Mother's in charge.

It really wasn't a march. It was more like a shuffle. There were four or more parallel, and at least 10 cross blocks stuffed with cheerfully indignant citizens who were all saying, "Oh, hell no," in the most vibrant and creative ways. At first, no one was sure what direction to walk, but eventually, we found a collective rhythm and faced the same direction.

There seemed to be equal numbers of women and men of all ages, children, and the occasional dog. I later heard that buses and trains were stopped en route due to the crowd, so people jumped out and marched where they were.

Each exhibit space came with a 10x10 tent, so we brought miles of red fabric, a rug, plenty of comfy pillows to lay on, electric candles, and a bowl of chocolate candy for the altar. The tent was enclosed on all four sides. The energy outside was electric and the air was filled with a thick layer of advocacy and power-driven chants, songs, and clever and hilarious homemade signs. But step inside the red tent to a sacred place where, depending on the moment, you would find women singing, meditating, crying, laughing, or quietly talking with new sisters. Stepping in from the high energy of the streets North and South, East, and West into a space where the energy flowed in a spiral was magical. Some women came and left, and a few young women stayed all day. One homeless woman joined us and we filled her pockets with chocolate before she left. I brought three bags of chocolate. Women were helping themselves to the bowl all day long. When it was time to pack up, I found the bowl still had plenty of chocolates with two unopened bags still stashed away.

We were among more than four million people on planet Earth facing the same direction, with not one recorded act of violence, energized by the same sacred enough-ness. In the center was a red tent holding space for us all.

Archetypes are like the riverbeds,
which dry up when the water deserts them,
which it can find again at any time."

~Carl Jung

Meeting Your Maiden, Mother, Crone

The only sure thing about a woman's life is her blood flow. Unless she has had a hysterectomy or has an otherwise unusual medical reason, she bleeds, and her womb comes into its purposeful existence to give and sustain life and wisdom. Evidence is found in the universal truths of the phases of the moon and what Goddess cultures call Blood Mysteries with the cornerstones of Maiden, Mother, and Crone.

According to some earth-based and Goddess cultures, this is a philosophy of the specific phases of a woman's life that show up characteristically. While some emphasize the relativity to a woman's blood flow, others relate to the moon cycle as it circles Earth; the new moon, the waxing crescent, the full moon, and the waning crescent. No matter how we relate the common characteristics, we cannot discount that these stages of our bodies are majestic and God-gifted life cycles. They are evidence that our life progresses with a natural purpose and as a process of defining and guiding us. The Maiden, Mother, and Crone archetypes are very important to pay attention to on our Liminal Odyssey to know which archetype is driving us through the Hero's Journey.

An archetype is the avatar of our highest ideals of a particular framing of a personality, culturally specific to that personality, persona, and identifiable characteristics. There is no one model of any one of the mythical archetypes, but strong attributes and qualities are consistent. In Goddess culture, those archetypal and mythical figures are important to all men and women so we can wrap our minds around what to identify with. Jesus is a great example of such an archetype, as are the mythical messiahs since early civilization.

The Maiden is the cycle of life when a young girl gets her first blood flow. Her womb comes into its sacred purpose, and she enters into the life-giving force of nature. In many indigenous cultures today, the ritual of this rite of passage is celebrated by taking the first drops of blood outside and giving them to Earth as an offering, paying honor, or a number of other culturally significant explanations of which I am not qualified to elaborate on in that I am not an indigenous person, or at least one with that culture.

Her womb is now preparing for the natural process upon which all human life depends. Characteristics of a Maiden are vulnerability, adventure, spontaneity, freedom to follow curiosity, play, and fearlessness. Her body's transformation is exquisite in its holy design, and she should be sprinkled with flowers and danced around in joyful ceremony.

The Mother is the second official stage of a woman's life, associated with the next phase of blood flow, the womb's purpose, which enlists a whole new set of conditions, insights, wisdom, and activating characteristics.

The act of accepting responsibility and responsiveness to another's needs was right on target in the birthing of a new chapter of a Liminal Odyssey. The awareness of it in the moment is not always present, but it, itself, is. In fact, the ability to accept and surrender to it, is nature's way of protecting the next seven generations, maybe even the survival of our species. It is supposed to come naturally. A byproduct of this stage is a shift in the ego's purpose. She can surrender in her confidence to care for others despite repercussions because it means doing the right thing for their safety and protection. She's responsive, selfless and she can do hard things, like stick her hand in a gross garbage disposal to retrieve a favorite toy.

Just because the womb now becomes an incubator for a new life force, child or childless, does not mean the Maiden qualities are not still at play. They constantly reappear and dance with the Mother because it is who she is and that does not go away; it just continues to be layered upon like new rings of a tree as she grows. The rings tell her story, mark her age and growth, yet, to suggest this process is linear is to lose the very essence of the woman in her entirety.

Like Indra's Net, it's when the patterns start making sense to us that we can accept our Crone initiation. As the third stage of the Triple Goddess archetype, the Crone is the culmination of a life lived through the other two stages: Maiden and Mother. If I wore t-shirts with sayings on them, mine would say, "Crone in Training," or "I want to be a Crone when I grow up." Her blood flow stops but remains in the womb as her spiritual nutrient, containing in it a life of wisdom from lessons learned.

At some point, one comes to realize she has earned the miles to claim this place as hers and hers alone, meaning she alone stands barefoot on this holy ground. If she tells everyone she's arrived, she needn't take her shoes off, because she's not quite there yet. It's a sacred place and both Maiden and Mother are woven into the fabric of who she is so brightly that she can be all at once with a joy-full, wise, and buoyant heart. She has the freedom to be unattached, yet knows the value of holding on tightly to the things that matter most. It is sacred, soaked with every moment of her life, now honored for the culmination of every moment that has come before, creating a self that has her own thumbprint, birthmark, personal ID coding of no other before now, or ever, for time immemorial.

There's nothing more delightful than a win-win-win collaboration. Everyone is satisfied, appreciated, and mutually benefits from the outcome. Everyone brings their own unique tone, quality, and skill set. When we answer the call after the first invitation, it means the Sisters MMC (Maiden, Mother, Crone) are singing to us in perfect harmony. It is a harmonizing experience because it engages the vulnerability, adventure, spontaneity, freedom, curiosity, play, courage, and/or fearlessness of the Maiden; responsiveness, selflessness and/or self-awareness of the Mother, and confidence, wisdom, and freedom of the crone. Through the lens of Gary's Multisensory Human perception, a new magic emerges. It is as if they have been in rehearsals for decades, because they have, and are now in tune.

When Motown first began making hits, artists like The Temptations and The Supremes would travel together in buses around the country on tour, taking the stage, one after the other. Occasionally they performed together. The tour of our life is no different. The Temptatious Multi-senses and Supreme MMC each harmonize and make memorable music as solid gold artists. When they take the stage together, they blow the roof off any stadium, including the Rose Bowl. When they arrive, we needn't ask questions, just open the door and get out of their way, or pitch a red tent and say, "Yes."

I would hate to think that anyone would dare suggest they have not had moments of pure unadulterated solid gold sensations. The sensation is one of joy and feels as though the stars have all showed up at once to light up our life. It was the same feeling we had when we pitched our red tent. It was crone-inspired and fulfilled. This is what the crone does: she holds sacred space, and it is one of her finest qualities.

According to the teachings of the Mayan Calendar and taught to me by one of the founding 13 Indigenous Grandmothers, Grandmother Flordemayo, we are entering the era of I'x (pronounced eēsh). I'x is a day identified by the symbol of a jaguar on the circular 20-day cycle of the Mayan calendar. The jaguar represents the spirit of feminine agility, tranquility, strength, power, wisdom, speed, and gazelle-like finesse of her gait as she maneuvers through her environment. Her spots represent the cosmos. She is feminine, hear her roar. Yet, the word *feminine* does not apply to gender but to the qualities of both male and female biological makeup and is dominant in the female animal by the simple fact that we give birth and are predisposed with hormones that keep us and our children safe and nurtured for our survival with all the innate qualities of a jaguar, the ultimate crone.

It was not lost on me that Jaguar Shaman showed up in the process of writing this book.

Mayan wisdom and most indigenous cultures, scientific research, mysticism, Marilyn McCoo and The 5th Dimension, or a simple knowing, proclaims we are moving into the Age of Aquarius and have been for quite a while now.

To be clear, men can embody crone qualities. In fact, it's my humble but confident feeling that they all do, but it has been socialized out of them. I know many men who are perfect expressions of a deep abiding wisdom and divine feminine qualities, including Clay Boykin who holds sacred space in his organization Circles of Men Project. However, there is an unmistakable energetic flow that is distinct in the female body that can only really be experienced, and non-scientifically proven, in a sacred circle of women. When one man joins the circle, it's good and lovely, but it is different. Clay has shared that he has witnessed the energy change when a woman enters a men's circle.

Clay has been a friend and a colleague in the field of compassion and gender equity for years. In Clay lies a safe and trusted ally in making sense of a paradigm shift in relationships, leadership, and culture. He is a pioneer in exploring what he describes as the new compassionate male; the archetypal standard he identifies on the horizon. It is breathtaking to watch him navigate this new frontier through curiosity and humility. Clay and I have had discussions on many occasions, and agree that, as a step towards bringing women and men together for healing, there is a time for women to gather with women as in the red tent, and for men to gather with men in a sacred circle to address their unique healing needs. Separately, this enables men with men and women with women to learn how to fully embrace both their divine masculine and divine feminine energies Carl Jung referred to as the *anima* (female energy within men), and *animus* (male energy within women).

With over 200 S.A.R.A.H. sacred circles, the majority in my family room, and a handful with some male guests, the dynamic shift is clear. Because our bodies are literally the life-giving and nurturing Earth embodied, we share a heartbeat and a knowing that is unique to the female body. We are nature, yet over millennia we have been socialized to distance ourselves from that fact; like a slow drip over centuries, water can carve a tunnel into a solid rock.

When I got my first period, my mother slapped my face, not to punish me, but as a rite of passage. The story was that this was a tradition passed down and a ritual for generating blood flow that my body was losing. But it felt more like a ritualistic slap in the face that I was now something dirty. For some reason, it was my reaction to my daughter's own rite of passage. I did not know what else to do in that moment. I am guilty as charged for passing down a patriarchal custom. The slap stops with her.

In observant Islamic and ultra-conservative Jewish cultures, a man will not touch a woman since he is not sure she is *kosher* (meaning, if she is bleeding, she's not clean). In places today such as Ethiopia and Northern Nepal, women are sent to a menstrual hut where they are cast out of their communities and, unlike the gift from nature bestowed upon us, we are shamed and sequestered. Many women bring their young children with them. This cultural norm is often the cause of death from exposure, dehydration, snake bite, and smoke inhalation.

The idea of having a hut to retreat to is a philosophy worth holding onto. It is what Anita Diamant was driving home with her book *The Red Tent*. In a Red Tent, women choose to join their sisters during their moon cycle. This is where we reclaim our sacred nature and sisterhood in a space that is not available anywhere else. We can lose our bras and everything that does not serve us, sit in circle or dance in a frenzy. We can pet one another's hair to calm nerves, or cry in each other's laps. The Red Tent is also where women come to give birth and midwife both life and death. It's a sacred space and becomes a womb for women's wholeness in our most sacred time, the new moon.

We have been duped by patriarchy's hypnotic charms over centuries to believe we are separate from such natural mimicry. It's time to wake up and take another look. Dr. Riane Eisler, PhD, author of *Sacred Pleasure, The Real Wealth of Nations*, and *The Chalice and The Blade* refers to this phenomenon of cultural toxicity as The Domination Trance. Over millennia we have been socialized out of our connection to the spirit of the journey of life when we commoditized Earth. All that looking down at what we could take from Her meant we were not looking up and dreaming, honoring the cosmos and the mysterious. (By "we" I refer to most of modern-day civilization, because the traditional indigenous and earth-based cultures, foundationally, never lost their connection and have socially suffered the consequences.)

The cost of Spirit showing herself has proven dangerous by the sheer fact that mental health crisis is a pandemic and why "Trauma-Informed Therapy" is now a part of our lexicon. It's time for a cultural shift, and it's a good thing we are in one right now. How we show up for it depends on how we navigate our journey.

We are at a fascinating place now in the history of the human epoch where we are at the threshold of the next paradigm shift, which requires we re-member our relationship to our natural world, resulting in a Liminal Odyssey for the ages.

To navigate this shift of understanding and living into the Odyssey takes a measure of confidence, which is rooted in trust; the safety net to suspend freely in one's imagination. We know we are there because we are rattled with uncomfortable, complicated, and inconvenient decisions to make, and with no savior, wizards, or fairy godmothers in sight. We are forced to form new neuropathways that redirect and repave our belief system towards worthiness, confidence, and trust, and mend the gaping hole in our safety net.

Because we have choice, we can remember and practice our skills to carve new neuropathways to recall that we are the ones we are waiting for.

We forgot who we are, yet it is always there in hiding. It comes out sideways over millennia in the arts: poetry, song, dance, journaling, and mythology. That spirit never left us. It simply went underground, appearing in a clever cloak so as not to offend the patriarchy, at least right to its face. The Greeks did their part, originating the philosophies of psychology. In fact, the word, "psyche" is Greek for "soul," yet we still don't fully get it in mainstream society.

I won't spend much energy here on the church's role in this, but historical markers such as the Christian Inquisition is well-presented in the documentary *The Burning Times*, a must-watch. It is safe to say that the medieval era is responsible for the heavily patriarchal and fear-based society we are emerging from, requiring more and more midwives. I suspect that may be you, and possibly why you chose this book.

Goddess worship and the medicinal gifts of Earth were punishable acts by death, and men who connected to the divine feminine, until recently, have been highly demonized. Pagan culture has stepped out from behind the curtain and witches are literally coming out of the broom closet, as mainstream and rigid religious groups are losing youth by the droves. For decades now the growing religious identity of the western world is "none."

The growing popularity of Goddess culture over the past three decades, especially the past several years, means the psyche of humanity is in need of some crone wisdom and the Goddesses are the personification of that in action. The multitude of crises today seems to be of biblical proportions, including the plague. Yes, we can hear it if we listen closely, Mother's in charge and the Goddesses, our archetypal sheroe's are being called to the front line. They possess a fiercer kind of enough-ness; one that is not patriarchal or dominating; one that is direct, and clear, strong and unwavering in her Love.

It's said that the older we get, the louder the crone's voice gets, but I believe it's our ears that are more attuned to hearing the voice that has been whispering to us from the shadows our entire lives. We were simply not ready to hear it. We had more work to do and more threads to follow; more mistakes and stumbles to experience; more synchronicities to notice; more gems and rocks to pick up. The more we tune in, the more we shine a light on that shadow until it's our illuminating primary operating system that drives our life. Then we have reached our full crone glory in living color and bright lights.

Responding to the call to open the front door at age 41 or popping up a Red Tent at 56 had nothing to do with my age. I was somewhere between Mother and Crone stages of life in terms of my blood flow, but you will never hear me suggest I am the latter. When I get there, I will have no need to impress you, and to suggest it would be Goddess heresy. However, it's worth mentioning here, because these acts are indicators that the condition of the crone was in rare form, and I can own that. I expect we all own moments when we responded to our soul's calling and did a good job at listening. The reality is, it was my collective five senses that determined my impulses. I take credit for saying, "Yes."

A crone also knows when to say, "No." The moment we find ourselves at the line in the sand, we can feel it in our body. If we are paying attention, we must pause, then listen our soul into a condition of discovery and disclosure, getting it closer to freedom each time.

When we are facing what appears as a monster or obstacle of another species, look again. It's just an old familiar friend, The Place of No Return. It can be scary, but because ultimately it means our soul's freedom, we take one for the team. I was 17 when I first met that line, and the choice was made for me. In that case, the will was stronger than the intention to return to destructive comfort. My crone showed up in a cape and knee-high boots and was my shero in the crisis of heartbreak.

Recognizing which of our Maiden, Mother, and Crone characteristics are present in any given situation is quite helpful, if not essential, in navigating the Liminal Odyssey. The moment we stop and check in, listen care-fully, and realize which of the three, or combination thereof are present, we are now in a liminal space. What we do next is the question of how our Odyssey will flow.

間

Seven
Abracadabra: The Sacred Integrity of Our Creation

*Our job is not to find God, but to clear the obstacles that
prevent us from the spiritual awakening
that leads us there.*

~ Michael Singer, *Untethered Soul*

My first experience at a Parliament of the World's Religions was in 2009 in Melbourne, Australia. A reported 10,000 people from every corner of the world attended, representing close to every religion, belief system, and culture. As with past Parliaments, each is held in a different location a few years apart.

Hundreds of workshops, a plethora of exhibits, expressions of cultural dance, chanting, art, and ritual filled the Melbourne Convention Center for seven days. People wearing their traditional regalia from their native lands created a carnival for the senses just walking to the bathroom. The original people and nations of the host country always open and close the event and tend the sacred fire that burns around the clock for the entire week. The Dalai Lama's monks create a sand mandala over the course of the week, one grain of colorful sand at a time in a symmetrically perfect pattern, only to take this masterpiece down to the river's edge on the last day and ceremoniously dump the sand into the water, demonstrating the impermanence of all things.

Presenters of global notoriety like Jane Goodall, Desmond Tutu, Marianne Williamson, the Dalai Lama, high-ranking government officials, and thought leaders are a given as plenary speakers and could also be found sitting next to you in a workshop. Since the 2004 Parliament in Barcelona, Spain, the local Sikh community fed us lunch each day. That's right. 10,000 people line up and are served the most delicious Indian cuisine every day for seven days, for free of course, in what is called a *langar*. (The Golden Temple in Amritsar, India, a Sikh *gurdwara* (place of worship) serves the hungry over 50,000 meals a day, every day of the year.)

Over the past four Parliaments, besides sitting in a myriad of transformational workshops, I have presented, led workshops, produced events, and had countless planned and spontaneous conversations. But it was the chance meetings while taking breaks in the hallways that were the juiciest and spirit-led meetings where I consistently find my next muse, mentor, or BFF.

It was on one of those breaks that I found room on a bench in the main hall and sat down next to six Jain nuns. I noticed as one approached us that she was lightly sweeping her path with a Wallis Tambo sweep broom, made of reeds. I asked their interpreter to explain what she was doing. With a neatly folded napkin to her mouth, she told me the primary tenet of Jainism, one of the oldest religions in the world dating back to 600 CE, is *ahimsa*, the fundamental principle to do no harm, and is one of the five sacred vows devout Jains take. Sweeping her path means that she is taking careful precautions not to step on a living being. I then asked her to explain the napkin she held to her mouth, as I noticed they were all conversing with one another in the same fashion. She told me that just as our feet have the capacity to do harm, so does our breath and our words. Of course, I had to ask her how they got to Melbourne from India. She told me they got special permission from their leadership to board and fly in an airplane and drive in a car.

It is not widely known that the expression "Abracadabra" comes from the Hebrew derivation *ebrah k'dabri*, meaning, "I create as I speak." Our words have the power to create or destroy. It's not too far of a stretch from the image of a 10-year-old magician waving a plastic wand in a figure 8, finishing the dramatics with a snap of the wrist and proclaiming his power to manifest a new reality.

I can have a sharp tongue, and while I have a long wick, at a point it catches a spark and once that happens, a forest fire is as good as blazing. I pity the representative on the phone who missed her training on good customer service. I do practice apologizing to them in such occurrences, which is much harder than it sounds. While keeping my words impeccable is not always a reality, the visual of a napkin over my mouth helps. Maybe when I reach full crone, I will have cleaned up that shortcoming. Until then, or to expedite the process, a broom, attached to a belt loop sweeping behind me reminds me of the opportunity (and responsibility) to clean up my messes. Greg definitely swept up his in his final stage of his Hero's Journey, the resurrection.

In addition to Grandmother Flordemayo, I have had the good fortune of spending a fair amount of time with Great Grandmother Mary Lyons, an Ojibwe elder whom I first experienced from the front row of a massive audience at the Inaugural Women's Assembly of the Parliament of World's Religions in Salt Lake City in 2015. Sitting (literally) at her hem, we all broke out in a massive applause when she shook her finger at the world religions and proclaimed, "Shame on You." I knew I was witnessing one bad-ass Grandmother.

Since then, we have hosted Great Grandmother on several S.A.R.A.H. programs and I have had more than a few personal conversations with her. When explaining why she prefers to be called "Great Grandmother" she says, "According to the great protocol of the original people, we carry the past seven generations and future seven generations within us. Each one of us sits at the center as a bridge as a great grandmother and holds the balance."

While both Grandmother Flordemayo and Great Grandmother Mary carry within them a profound knowledge base, deep spiritual wisdom, and an untouchable intelligence, they will sit on the floor with you and giggle. Their humility is breathtaking, especially when they are silly.

In fact, and largely because of the past six years that I have known and spent time with Grandmother Flordemayo, along with her genuine and dynamic daughter Heather Hall-Dudney Stone, I have experienced a model of humanity of the most generous standards. They give of their relationships and resources generously, but most valuable is the immeasurable wisdom they impart. They say it does not come from them. Instead, they are channeling the ancestors, which is substantial when we multiply each of these women by 15 (seven before and seven after with them in the center). I have experienced this with Grandmothers Jyoti Ma, SaSa, Barbara, and every Grandmother they have called into my life.

Great Grandmother Mary told me to take my two fingers and place them on the pulse of my neck. She said, "In that pulse are all those who have come before you and all who are to be." That responsibility under my fingertips brought me to my knees and has been a source of strength and courage since that conversation.

The cadence of language that is indicative of original peoples of North America is one of clarity, and rather simplistic. While their wisdom cannot be learned by textbooks, in a shamanic-knowing-kind-of-way, it comes from the cosmos and ancestors. The language's edges are sharp with no inflection. The rhythm is thought-full and care-full. Theirs is a distinct accent that is more than a dialect. It has intentional qualities. Great Grandmother tells me, "My father taught us to explain yourself as though speaking to children so they can clearly understand you. In this way, your words are impeccable and true." She went on to teach me about the ancient story of the 7 Grandfathers Teachings, known to be foundational to indigenous people's life.

In short, seven Grandfathers watched over humanity from the heavens. They noticed the destruction and suffering, poor behavior, and lack of harmony. So, they sent a messenger who could teach the values of Wisdom, Love, Respect, Bravery, Honesty, Humility, and finally Truth, which is to know all of these. As well, all seven of these values must be upheld together. None can be left out.

Like the collective senses of the Multisensory Human, when these seven values are upheld together, they create a condition of integrity. When we are in our integrity, how we present ourselves with our daily behaviors, the products we purchase, the manner in which we treat others (including the invisible irritant of a phone solicitor), the choices we make, how we honor our humanness, and the clarity of our words will be external expressions of will in perfect balance with intention. This, I call *grace*. And this is preparation for the most important parts of our Liminal Odyssey.

Impeccability and Grace

Whether an aerospace equipment manufacturer, a medical laboratory, or any contaminated space that requires a hazmat suit, a clean room is required to isolate the contaminant properly and safely. There must also be a process to keep damaging elements out with an effective cleansing procedure. When one leaves the contaminated area, before stepping foot into the general work environment, or out into the world, they must pass through the clean room and lock the sealed door behind them, strip their protective gear, leaving all the impurities, toxins, and poisons behind, like a good industrial strength Clorox rinse. When they step out, they are impeccably clean and free of what they were carrying that did not serve them. They are not carrying any of the old muck to where they are going next.

Similar to a baby's birth, leaving the cozy darkness of the only reality it has known into a new way of being, going from one environment to another, is natural, necessary, scary, and can be very messy. And, not unlike these changing times, if you have ever given birth, it hurts like hell. No one really knows what it will be like when we get into the light, with a new awareness, culture, and way of breathing and being in the world. We hold onto the comfortably familiar and resist change. However, we have no choice but to clear the muck, because we are heading in that direction, regardless if we are ready or not.

Some feel we have just begun the morning sickness and bloating. Others feel we are in the birth canal, complete with painful contractions and expansion of body parts that don't normally stretch that far. Many in my circles believe we have arrived. The first thing that the doctor and nurses do after the umbilical cord is cut is to clear the baby's breathing passage and body of residue that no longer serves her. She is officially on the other side, clean, and with a fresh start in a new reality.

This new epoch is, in the immortal lyrics popularized and performed by The 5th Dimension, one of "harmony and understanding, mystic crystal revelation, and no more falsehoods and derisions," ensuring we leave our falsehoods and condition of derisions behind and are ready for a clean delivery. Making sure we did not bring any residual muck with us not only applies to the individual, but to society as a whole to prepare ourselves for the new world we are co-creating. The muck is an illusion anyway. Maybe it's just the mischievous pixies trying to trip us up and test us. With awareness and will, they don't stand a chance.

I had accepted my marching orders, met my mentors and fairy godmothers, worked on the cleansing process, and now I was rounding the opening of an unknown place with a one-way ticket. The question is, would I be an obstacle of what is inevitable, or become its midwife?

In the book *The Four Agreements*, by don Miguel Ruiz, we learn about the agreement to keep our words impeccable. We must be clear on what we want, and what we want to convey with clarity and power in the direction of love.

Keeping our words and deeds impeccable is a worthy goal. The moment this agreement sunk in, I realized how easy it is to catch myself from expanding the truth, either inflating or deflating it. I do not lie, and practice not stretching the truth for dramatic appeal. I learned this is a condition of not feeling worthy enough and once I realized that, I stopped. I also practice not saying "I am sorry" as a passing statement unless I owe an apology and even then, my sentiments are far more sincere.

I prefer to thank someone for their patience or their sense of humor if I goof. Women say those three words way too often without realizing they are discounting their own power and the deep patriarchal roots associated with feeling "wrong" for the slightest of movements.

One of the most liberating feelings is that of being in one's truth, and I like that feeling so much, it's been graduated from an agreement to hard-fast rule. It's also the best chance at getting what we want and/or pray for. When I got clear and impeccable with what I was looking for, it created an entirely new perspective and crystal-clear picture so I could ask the right question with integrity. Then he appeared and exceeded my imagination. Being genuine with integrity and self-awareness means we are speaking our truth, which might just manifest our wildest dreams.

I depend on pure honesty and candor, and when someone's truth is delivered with clarity, and better, with a touch of kindness, I know it is a truth I have the privilege of hearing. I do not have time for tap dancing and side show antics to get a point across. I just do not have the time to figure it all out and read between the somersaults. Just tell me your truth with integrity and then we are both clean and clear and I get to grow, or not. Who has time for the tip-toing and carnival act to save my feelings? Come at me with a bullhorn and nothing gets solved, and I don't think anyone really feels better after that. Either you are not clear on what you want to express, it is not rooted in love and/or your integrity, or you are trying to save my feelings, none of which is helping either of us one little bit. So, share with me your power because you love me and want me to hear your wisdom and insight. I only want loving, supportive, and genuine relationships. And if every one of my relationships does not resemble that description, a good question I ask myself is, "Why?" and what needs to be cleaned and/or cleared to live an authentically healthy and joy-full life.

Some believe this transitionary time explains the piling-on of crises happening all around us on just about every level. As these words are being written, we are amid the Covid-19 pandemic, extreme climate changes, rising waters, deforestation, and the crashing of political systems. We are also seeing humanity more divided, self-soothing and self-preserving at the expense of others. It can all be overwhelming, and many are experiencing the collective anxiety that is in the air causing emotional issues that can't quite be nailed down. Besides doing my best to be environmentally and politically responsible, sometimes the best I can do is check myself for bugs in my integrity system, walk through the decontamination channel, and pull out the Clorox rinse when I make a mess.

Dropping into the liminal spaces for inquiry, listening and honoring our sacred nature, then behaving in the direction of our integrity is when we are living from our spick and span authentic power. It is then we begin the process of re-membering our body and working within its system, which is designed to support our bliss and well-being.

Eight
Heart-Shaped Evidence

The most important instrument in an orchestra is the tuning fork.

~ Marc Ian Barasch

"I am building a mandala in my front yard, and I am asking each of my friends to contribute a rock." Ruth Broyde Sharon is known by many as the single most inquisitive person alive. Her interest in what lies in between the liminal seams of your story may derail you, but she is mastered in the art of unpacking the real story. There is a rarity to Ruth. Her candid curiosity is deeply rooted in a sincere intention to understand the very essence of the gifts she is excavating. Ruth is a unique example of the saying, "Look and you shall find," and Ruth is looking for the heart of every story, situation, and place. This quality enables her to manifest the events and initiatives she produces with a depth that is thought-full and stretches the edges of what is possible for world peace, like her 2-volume masterpiece, *Interfaith, the Musical*. She has been my friend, confidant, truth-teller, advisor, and a spiritual mentor for nearly 20 years. She has also been a model of interfaith community building and has served in leadership at S.A.R.A.H. since we began our journey.

"I can do better than that!" I said, and off I went to the rockiest beach in Southern California to find "the one." While my husband parked himself on a blanket with a bag of Cheetos, I started at the waterline.

About two years earlier, my then 10-year-old son Matthew emerged from around the bend where our boat was anchored in a cove on Lake Mohave with a gift of hearty proportions. We spent every summer playing on the lake, including long days of either jet-skiing, inner tubing, or just sitting in a secluded cove doing nothing together. The quiet never got old. We had a radio but rarely turned it on. Matthew took off around the corner on an exploration and returned with a gift for me; a stone that was a perfectly symmetric-shaped heart.

I took it home, found a small plate holder for it and placed it on the shelf, right in-between two awards I had received for my community work. But this was the greatest of all awards; an expression of love from my son who saw a heart and thought of me.

Later that summer while on vacation, I decided to see if I could find my own heart-shaped rock. The chant came to me, "Look and you shall find," until finally, there it was, my own discovery. I found a close-enough resemblance to a heart-shaped rock and put it in my pocket, feeling accomplished and having no idea what Matthew had begun.

Before I knew it, I had bowls filled with heart-shaped rocks in our family room. Most of them came from family or friends, or simply appeared in front of me as I was on a walk. When a friend was traveling and asked if I wanted anything from that country, I said, "Yes, please take some time and seek out a heart-shaped rock." I was hoping to receive such a souvenir to add to my collection as much as I was giving them the same thrill of seeking out and finding. Asking someone to think of me in the shape of a heart was an added motive.

Ghada, my fiery, hand-flaring bundle of passion and compassionate friend whom I had sat next to years earlier in that square-shaped circle in the mosque, had picked up what appeared to be a dime-sized heart-shaped rock while on a beach in Lebanon, only to turn it over to find it had a perfect heart-shaped fossil-like image on the other side.

When Mormon missionaries came to my home and I invited them in for lemonade and pita chips, they noticed my collection and I proceeded to share my well-rehearsed story of "Look and you shall find." Two weeks later those same young men reappeared at my door, with their bikes parked on the sidewalk, each of them with a heart-shaped rock they found for me. They only asked me not to tell anyone because they were supposed to be out doing their missionary duties. However, I reminded them that those duties included seeking and learning about the world. Mission accomplished in my book of Mormon.

They were outed anyway when my dear friend and Mormon (Church of Jesus Christ of Latter-Day Saints) Bishop Tom Thorkelson heard about this story and wrote an article for the Los Angeles Times about a Jewish woman who welcomed in two missionaries and the journey I inadvertently sent them on. He shared that soon afterward I had submitted a collection of those rocks to the County Fair and won a blue ribbon. Each rock was labeled with where it came from, including "Mormon Missionaries." More than 10 years later, Tom is still sharing that story with anyone within email radius.

It is important to know that I am Tom's favorite person on the planet, but he makes every single person he meets feel the same way. Tom typically introduces himself in interfaith meetings we are both at as, "A follower of the Worldwide Church of Sande".

Years later Tom and his wife Sheila were on an Alaskan cruise and while on a tour of a glacier, Tom insisted everyone in their excursion group find their friend Sande a heart-shaped rock. The consummate leader that he is, Tom assigned everyone a mission to seek and find. And they did. That stone is proudly on display in my entryway shelf. Taped to the back of it in Tom's handwriting, "Tom and Sheila." In writing this book, I reached out to Tom and Sheila and asked if they remembered the name of the glacier. Sheila responded, "Sure do! It was St. James Bay, July 13, 2018, at 10:40 AM!" Was Tom the Crazy Dancing Guy in the group? Or the First Follower? Did Tom start a glacier wave?

Ruth's request was received as an invitation to show off my talent of discovering a heart wherever I made up my mind to find it. I was on it and overconfident, at that. Bent at the neck, I began my chant, intentionally and slowly walking for half a mile up the beach, chanting and strolling, strolling and chanting. I believed, and that meant it shall come, right? Maybe not, but I did not stop believing. I found myself back where I began, near the place where my husband had now been napping. My neck was sore. I felt defeated. Then I remembered where I was and who I was standing in front of. She hadn't let me down before. So I turned and said, "Grandmother Ocean, please bring me a heart-shaped stone." As if waiting for me to ask, a small wave slowly approached, covered my feet up to my ankles, and slipped back quietly. I looked down. To the right of where I stood, there it was: a shiny, wet, perfectly shaped heart-shaped stone, just like the sand dollars and other assorted gifts she laid at my feet over my lifetime. I picked it up and held it in front of my eyes and proclaimed, "Thank you!"

In that moment, a little boy, probably around 10 years old, came bounding out of the ocean right in front of me. His eyes focused on this article of amazement I was holding up with an outreached arm and said, "Wow!" I asked him what he was referring to, wanting to know if we were thinking the same thing. Did he understand the majesty of it all? Was he looking at me, or beyond me to something else? He proclaimed, "A heart-shaped rock!" with an excitement as if this was the newest toy on the market and he wanted to be the first on his block to have one. I handed it to him. He held it in his hands and examined it closely. His face lit up. *Who is this kid?* I thought. I told him to give it to his mom, whom I assumed he was heading back to, and off he went.

I lowered my shoulders, sighed, and resumed position, bent at the neck, and the chant and exploration continued. Only this time, almost immediately, I found a heart-shaped rock, then another and another, all within a 5-foot radius of where I received the first. I pulled up my t-shirt to make a kangaroo pouch to carry 13 heart-shaped rocks back to where my husband was patiently waiting. About a month later I handed Ruth a gift bag filled with heart-shaped rocks for her mandala. I heard she never did get around to making one. It did not matter. I trust my angels put her up to asking the question anyway.

I never did ask my son where he found that heart-shaped rock.

Our awareness, assumptions, attitudes,
attention, alignment, actions and allowing
determine our frequency. They are our request to the Universe.

~ Andrew Cameron Bailey and Connie Baxter Marlow
The Trust Frequency: Ten Assumptions for a New Paradigm

The Trust Frequency

No matter what we are looking for, whether it's an answer to a nagging question, someone to share our love, or a heart-shaped rock, being clear with what we are asking is almost as important as trusting we will receive it.

I never doubt for a moment that I will find a heart-shaped rock when I start my search. I never know how long it will take but its discovery is always in Chronos time. However, the search for my answer that morning at the Rose Bowl continues to be answered in Kairos time and I trust more gems will appear as life unfolds, which means they will.

When we don't understand why situations are as they appear, or try to make sense of betrayal, disappointment, or unimaginable suffering, understanding the Trust Frequency can be more than comforting. It is empowering.

In their book *The Trust Frequency, Ten Assumptions for a New Paradigm*, Andrew Cameron Bailey and Connie Baxter Marlow writes, "When we apply a combination of acceptance and gratitude (which is not resignation) to determine our next steps, trusting that all is going according to plan despite appearances to the contrary, we find ourselves in a new reality."

Trusting the Universe has our back, always conspiring for the soul's highest purpose, no matter what meteors land on us is a tall order, but worth the work. To practice, I repeatedly recite Connie and Andrew's 10 Assumptions:

1. We live in a conscious loving Universe. Only Love exists.
2. The Universe loves us unconditionally.
3. We create reality through the power of our consciousness.
4. The 7 A's; Awareness, Assumptions, Attitude, Attention, Alignment, Action and Allowing determine our frequency and are our requests to the universe.
5. Free will is an absolute law of the Universe.
6. Circumstance guides us on our journey to wholeness.
7. There is only Now, this precious present moment.
8. All of creation is one.
9. Humanity is on an evolutionary upward spiral.
10. The Trust Frequency is available to anyone, anywhere, anytime.

It was the Trust Frequency that I was vibrating in while sitting in the otherwise uncomfortable stadium seat, stage left, the morning of June 6th, 1982. Apparently, the structure of the oval-shaped container of a football stadium served as a conductor to convert that vibration into kinetic energy, generated by the Universe's plan to free my soul.

I love that the most common word in a young child's vocabulary is, "Why?" I suggest we all practice listening to our inner child and ask ourselves that question about everything. Everything. Including this book. In this way, we can say we are in our integrity because we have taken the time to check ourselves at the door.

To trust requires vulnerability, or is it the other way around? In fact, they are partners. Vulnerability begs the question, *what could happen?* The old "why" comes in handy here. I have "why'd" myself right into a state of courage. I have asked one "why" after another until I ran into the real reason I was lacking trust. Pain or ego usually top the list. Yet, when I remember all that matters is knowing my truth, or what I am made of, who I am, or forgive my limitations, I am just fine. In fact, the worst-case scenario can occur, and I have the capacity to navigate through it with this skill in my tool bag. Applying Connie and Andrew's philosophy that everything is happening for us has been a lifeline for me and one of the most empowering tools I carry.

Nobody got here alone or without being influenced by another. On a Hero's Journey, mentors, models, and supporters are essential. Those who took us by the hand, often gently and with generosity and hospitality, are easy to recall and bow to. They imparted their wisdom, skills, connections, and perhaps their money upon us. They are the ones we seek out or welcome when they appear in our lives. Their support points us down the easy path because, where else would they send us? Naturally, we trust them and it's easy to be vulnerable with them.

Interestingly however, I have found the ones who created the most pain in my life, some of which started out as a mentor and/or friend whom I trusted dearly, and whose betrayal felt like a sock in the throat taking the wind out of me, were my most memorable allies. It took practicing asking why in the face of the betrayal over and over again until I discovered the gifts they gave me. The more I practice, the quicker the realization appears, now in record time.

In mythology or any movie plot, these characters are portrayed as evil and our enemies. This does not mean I look back at them now with affection, but I do not have disdain in my heart and can appreciate, and more greatly value, the lesson that is wrapped in the experience. I have yet to meet a so-called enemy whose lesson was not profound, or even remarkable in a small way. Not one. The guy who almost ran me off the road even taught me the lesson of control, focus, and respect for others who share the highway. The friend who started a business with me and ran off with our project in the dark of night did me the greatest service so my energies could be invested at S.A.R.A.H. At the time, these occasions of heartache and dissolution reeled me back to childhood trauma of abandonment, providing some major ugly-cry moments. There may be one or two in which I have yet to see the lesson, but I will keep seeking, asking why, and trust it will come.

I challenge everyone to pull up what felt like the worst experience in your life and find the multifaceted diamond in the center. You may not be ready to look and see it, but when you are, trust it will change everything, including your understanding of forgiveness.

One of my favorite workshops I give to kids and grownups alike is called *Make A Difference 101*. It's a fun-filled, interactive experience of compassionate action to make a point of the power of allies and community. In it, I tell this story of zebras in the Serengeti. The story I heard goes like this: Social scientists were studying the individual behaviors of pack animals, so they set up on a hill and watched a herd of zebras, day in, and day out. They were trying to follow individual behavior patterns, but they found that to be quite difficult since zebras all look exactly the same. It was impossible for them to do any true study since they could not single them out. So, a genius scientist got the bright idea to sneak up on a zebra and paint a red mark on its behind. (Actually, they tranquilized it with a gun first, but my rendition is far more imaginative of a scientist tiptoeing up to a herd in the dark of night with a pail of red paint, since I do not encourage animal cruelty for the sake of science.)

The next day, a lion was able to single out the zebra with a literal bullseye painted on its rump, chased it down and ate him. The scientists discovered something they hadn't planned. As a collective pack without individual distinction, the herd appeared to the lion as one massive animal. But single out the subject and now this unique singular one with an "eat me" sign on its rump is bite-sized and an inviting menu option. The end. Of course, this insults the circle of life, the Universal (and nature's) manner of maintaining balance and reciprocity of all creatures, but to make a point, here the scientists make it easy for the lion who is just doing her job. I take advantage of this fable to drive home this next point.

We are more powerful in our tribe and our community. So is fear. It's smart that way. It knows to collect all kinds of garments of guilt, doubt, shame, an illusion of a litany of embarrassing events, and cloaked in all kinds of protective gear to hide behind so it can thrive in our psyche and make one quiver, apologize, or worse: miss a gold-plated opportunity. Its goal is to make sure you do not trust anyone, or yourself.

Pull apart and mark the seemingly massive body of fear with a big red bullseye and you will have prepared something bite-sized that you can chew on. But I suggest blessing it for the opportunity to see it, and learn from it, and then taking it to the fire pit and releasing it into a cloud of smoke. (This is where it's important to remember the essential element of The Trust Frequency that all is in Love, even those who make us quiver.)

Clearing the smoke of fear is like clearing the throat. It's essential to be in pitch to live our most authentic and wildly wonderful life, no matter how we define it. It's ours to hold in trust, freedom, and joy.

"In 2015 I learned about a process of protocol and reconciliation from Hereditary Chief Phil Lane, Jr. Ihanktonwan, and Chickasaw Nations. It was only one of the deeply profound lessons I have been blessed to learn from him over the 10 years we have been friends, since I served in leadership at the United Religions Initiative for North America, and he was a Global Trustee.

His deeply spiritual intelligence, coupled with profound Indigenous knowledge and wisdom from his Dakota and Chickasaw lineages is often accompanied with a bellowing belly laugh to accentuate a serious and weighty truth. He has come to my aid more than a few times, reminding me to "put it in the fire," and let it go. It was out of a need to address some interpersonal issues that I learned about this protocol based on Indigenous knowledge and wisdom.

At S.A.R.A.H., we call it our *Agreements for Care and Caregiving* and consider it one of our foundational principles. This gave our *Ouch Policy* more structure and responsibility. It is a document we each agree to which states that in the event of any personal issues, we commit to stopping what we are doing and directly pulling aside the one we are having the issue with, followed by simple steps to ensure a healthy outcome, no matter what. It is critical that we agree in advance before there is any trouble in paradise. Because we operate in a state of trust, knowing we have this safety net, we can have more fun, be open and vulnerable, and especially, be wildly creative.

We know that our organization depends on new solutions to old problems, so that means we must be creative. Creativity and distrust cannot co-exist. The same is true for our commitment to having fun. We have a lot of fun, because we trust one another, and know that if anything goes awry, we have a safety net.

Over the past 20 years, we can count on one hand how many have left our organization in any condition other than in Love. The frequency of trust is a power almost as strong as Love. In fact, I cannot tell them apart.

This chapter cannot do justice to the power of The Trust Frequency, and I invite you to spend time with Andrew and Connie's book because I believe it's vitally important to your Liminal Odyssey.

Cultivating skills to apply the Liminal Odyssey to our life will be sorely discounted if we do not trust what we discover. Practicing sacred listening, acknowledging signs, allies, and synchronicities, and reconciling with difficult experiences serve us best when we trust ourselves enough to move in the direction that we have cleared. The Trust Frequency is possibly the most challenging and essential of all the skills we will find here. With it, our Liminal Odyssey can fully expand to its highest potential. Like every skill worth mastering, the more we practice it, the more it becomes an essential characteristic in our operating system.

Nine
Intergenerational Trauma and the Angel Corp

*The old ways are like freeze-dried
and we have to add the tears of our belonging and awareness
to make it all come to life.*

~ Rabbi Zalman Schachter-Shalomi, shared by Dr. Rabbi Tirzah Firestone

We were heading south by train to Washington Heights for an event I had flown to New York to attend. I was the guest of Deborah Moldow, whom I met through close friends, yet she and I had not had a single one-on-one conversation.

Deborah served as the Representative to the United Nations of May Peace Prevail on Earth International, and Director of the Evolutionary Leaders Circle. She's an interfaith minister with a sweet spirit and infectious laugh. She had invited me onto a panel at a UN event and presented at other events together with mutual friends, peace colleagues, and concentric circles, knowing one another for years. I had great admiration and felt a special warmth and love for her. While on a group call discussing an upcoming event, Deborah invited me to stay with her while I was in New York.

I love being with Deborah. She is very easy and made me feel comfortable. While driving to and from the train station, I noticed her raising her palm to either the driver's side or passenger window. At first, I figured she was just making a point in the discussion and then I realized she was blessing each body of water we were passing by or over.

"I don't understand why the same patterns of relationship breakdowns continue," I said as I was staring out the window of the train traveling into the city through a side of New York I had never seen before. We were talking about the various peace organizations and leaders thereof that we both knew, and some with whom I had experienced difficult relationships and even traumatic drama.

A pregnant moment passed, and then Deborah literally jumped off the bench seat we shared to redirect her body facing mine and said, "I know why I wanted you to stay with me! I have a message for you from my spirit guides!" The message was just delivered as an All-Points Bulletin! She must report this to me immediately. I pointed my knees towards her and listened carefully.

"You have some trauma work to do. Something happened to you as a child, or possibly your ancestral past, that continues to repeat itself in your behaviors and hang-ups, and resurfaces in your relationships, like a pulled weed's roots that never fully get unearthed." She instructed me to connect with that child or ancestor where trauma happened, to light a candle, and to ritualize the process of asking questions to my ancestors for healing. In that moment, Deborah's words tossed me on a trajectory that led me into deep dives and more gaping liminal spaces to navigate.

Our Ancestors, Allies, and Angels

That ability to receive a sense of knowing and respond to it, speaks volumes about a level of trust and connectedness to Source that Deborah embodies. To have such reverence and respect for that tap on the shoulder, to take action in any given direction, and then face that direction and proceed into the wind is a practice and discipline until it becomes a natural art. Deborah is a master at the art of listening and saying, "Yes" to that tap.

While listening to Source comes with a lot of practiced awareness, I am only now hearing and feeling it more and more, yet I can give a certification course on saying, "Yes." This is largely why I have a number of stories to tell thus far in my 60 years of life. Following the Yes is never a waste of time. The path it sets us upon is full of potential, new stories, new allies, new models and insights, and new forests of life-giving potency.

First, one must learn to recognize the tap on the shoulder, hear the whispers, or often the mega-watt clarion call. I was gifted with this power as a child to say, "Yes," but never got the memo that it was okay to say, "No." Because discernment was not a skill I was introduced to, I self-imposed a lot of treacherous terrain, like putting a fire hose in my hand and spending the first part of my life learning how to wield its power without drowning. Yet, that terrain has proven adventurous and has been fruitful enough to tell some fantastic stories. While I do not suggest ignoring opportunities for discernment, should you find yourself on the side of a regrettable or otherwise "not so wise" choice, in retrospect, turn it into a Liminal Odyssey and hold on. I bet you will find some juicy discoveries and experiences you would have otherwise missed.

The glaring in-your-face red lights, tire-piercing spikes thrown on the road to warn me not to pass, or the gauntlet of spinning razor-sharp circular blades and revolving fire torches unfortunately never stopped me. Thankfully, I can look back and see them as lessons.

The reason I can tell these stories and their relativity is because I stepped over the spikes and ran through the fire since I assumed that was what courage looked like. I am not sure if I was right or wrong, but I sure could have benefitted from the skill of discernment. Yet, while some lessons were avoidable, none were wasted. I can reconcile and know every ignored obstacle led me to Peace Sunday and every journey I have yet to take.

What Deborah shared with me took me on an Odyssey of unpacking intergenerational trauma that I was repeating and living in. It also helped me to realize my army of angels, or what is more like my personal Angel Corps who have mutual contractual duties with other's angels. Deborah and her angels were simply following orders. Now they were high-fiving each other because their mission was accepted and underway.

I began the regular "check-in" process over a lit candle and sitting in meditation with my ancestors. I quickly distilled the pattern of relationships down to the essence of trust. While I had already read *The Trust Frequency*, and referred to it many times, it began to make a new kind of sense to me.

I found myself on the playground of Pt. Vicente Elementary school in second grade feeling alone. I remembered the feeling of having to live up to the best version of myself because I was one of only a few Jewish kids in the entire school. Kids approached me to feel horns on top of my head or insist I could not be Jewish because I did not have a big nose. I gave away my lunch money to prove Jews were not cheap. Is this where not trusting my authentic self began? Was I more concerned with representing the entire Jewish race than being me and trusting I was enough? Was this condition implanted in my cellular memory by a lineage of people who could not trust anyone or the Nazis would surely find them? I could literally go back to the enslaved Hebrews of the Egyptians. Indeed, I inherited a heavy load and if I was serious about lightening up, I had some work to do.

I began to ritualize the traumas, asking my ancestors for help to engineer and lay the new foundation for the construction of a new thought highway to be carved in my brain. Sure enough, they answered the cry for help.

Two years later, I co-created an online Passover seder with author Dr. Riane Eisler, and with help from friend, recording artist, and music producer Aliza Hava and Rabbi Paula Marcus, convened two more profound women leaders: Starhawk and Rabbi Dr. Tirzah Firestone who joined us to co-produce our program. It was all a divine orchestration to introduce me to Rabbi Tirzah whose book *Wounds Into Wisdom, Healing Intergenerational Jewish Trauma* and workshop was just what my ancestors had planned for me. I later signed up for her course, *Finding Healing and Resilience in Ancestral Wisdom, Release the Trauma, Lineage and Change the Direction of Your Legacy*, where, with practical tools and insightful information, I could deepen my healing process in honor of my ancestors, my children, and the next generations.

Rabbi Tirzah led us through a process to reveal the patterns of our family's trauma and the conditions that we can easily trace, and some we cannot. Of course, there are conditions that we can easily trace to how we were raised, including the hang-ups and belief systems our parents planted in us and we watched in their actions. We default to those patterns of thinking until we start asking questions, like "How can I stop the cycle of poor choices and toxic relationships?"

When we trace the patterns in our own lives and those of our immediate family, and family of ancestors we never met but share a common branch with, we discover shared traits and experiences. While we can see that the buck was passed down through the branches, we can make the choice that it stops here. We don't have room for it in our luggage on the Odyssey. It only weighs us down and like airline luggage fees, could be expensive to bring it along.

Until then and along the way, I fumbled around in the dark. Now I was equipped to listen intently, follow clues and threads, pay a new kind of attention to my own behaviors and triggers that prepared me with skill-building capacity. Those skills and practical applications became the clinical lab for my education, and research to be tested.

The rituals to help evoke awareness of intergenerational trauma were working. Deborah and her angels were right on target. Suddenly, the angels started showing up regularly. More than show up, they came out from the floorboards, rafters, water lines, and thin air.

I always joked that I must have an army of angels protecting me in bubble wrap to explain how I have survived. I have so many protectors in fact that I dispatch them out to others when they are in need. I always call up my top angels, but the truth is, they are all Admirals, cream-of-the-crop, highly qualified and highly appointed.

Now I understand that those angels could be my ancestors who surround me to keep me from repeating patterns of their trauma as ingredients for my own. I put them to good use, too. Besides keeping them out of breath guiding and protecting me, I send them out on missions to help others I love.

I have found the best reaction to a friend in need is to dispatch my top angels to their side. They are there faster than I can finish my order requisite. They serve me well and the more I send out on missions of aid, the more they multiply. Nothing beats a warm hug from the protective wings of an angel on a mission.

I happen to believe that we should be careful not to accept all the credit for actions and choices we make that benefit others and ourselves. We can, however, honor ourselves for listening and learning over time so that we show up in a manner that serves and improves everyone's well-being.

Important to the cleansing process on our Liminal Odyssey is to clear, as best we can, the shadow-side characteristics that keep unhealthy behaviors in play. We can point a spotlight on them and address them with love and care. Considering the growing research on ancestral and generational trauma, we have access to a plethora of resources, videos, and books on the subject. Let's also not forget our honorable ancestral traits and gifts that deserve some dusting off and respect. Invite your ancestors' wisdom into your practice. Even if you do not know anything about them, they existed. They may be waiting for your invitation to join you, first-class, on your Liminal Odyssey.

Where your passions meet the needs of the world,
therein lies your calling.

~ Aristotle

Where your passions meet the needs of your soul,
therein lies your soul's freedom.

~ Sande Hart

Ten
Self-Realization and the Sacred Agreement

You may control a mad elephant;
You may shut the mouth of the bear and the tiger;
Ride the lion and play with the cobra;
By alchemy you may learn your livelihood;
You may wander through the universe incognito;
Make vassals of the gods; be ever youthful;
You may walk in water and live in fire;
But control of the mind is better and more difficult.

~ Paramahansa Yogananda, *Autobiography of a Yogi*

In June of 2015, I was invited to go to Lake Shrine, a property located in Southern California, constructed and dedicated by Paramahansa Yogananda, founder of the Self Realization Fellowship. A guru who came to the United States from India in the early 20th century, he brought the first yogic teachings to the Western world. He was, and still is, a well-respected and honored figure among scientists, physicians, theologians, and seekers. He has, and continues to transform the lives of millions, and most notably was brought to the mainstream by celebrities like Elvis Presley and George Harrison. Yogananda, or Yogiji as I refer to him affectionately, floated on each inch of the small lake on his land to bless its waters. His careful placement of each tree and plant was meticulous. 62 years later, visitors benefit from that loving intention, including me.

The first thing he created on this property was a memorial to Mahatma Gandhi which enshrines a small amount of his ashes gifted from the Gandhi family. It is the only place in the world to make that claim outside of India. Perched above a natural amphitheater of spiritual and mythical proportions sits a temple and a retreat center where I would experience my first five-day silent retreat.

The entire property sits just two blocks away from the Santa Monica State Beach with Pacific Coast Highway, a supermarket and a scattering of small businesses, residences, lots of tall trees, and a Chabad school in between. It quickly dawned on me how poetic it was that a silent retreat center sat in the center of a noisy and busy community, let alone above one of the most traveled coastal highways in America.

All of what I just described is a gross understatement to the history, splendor, and magic of this 10-acre heaven-on-Earth and the gravity of spirit to which Paramahansa Yogananda can be attributed.

To reserve a stay at Lake Shrine, one must have a phone interview to make certain you are spiritually inclined, and not planning on using the space for band practice or disruptions to the other guests. My presence would have an impact on the others, so it was important to ascertain if I would be an appropriate guest in a silent retreat environment that was limited to approximately 20 others. It is also when you are told the rules to being a retreatant:

Rule #1: Please honor our code of silence.
Rule #2: There are no other rules.

Each room is comfortable and most have a million-dollar view of the ocean and beach. Vegetarian meals are served three times a day in a dining room with oversized windows.

Other than practicing silence in group, or meditation circles, I had never been silent in a group of people doing nothing but eating and gazing, and my social animal instincts were flipping out. This was as unnatural a setting for me as a fish out of water. But I was very happy to be there. I was very tired. The invitation came from someone who witnessed me going through what felt like a major traumatic experience at the time, and by the looks of it, I could benefit from an opportunity for a little self-realization.

It was an easy drive from my home and within an hour of arriving I heard the lunch gong summoning the retreatants to the dining room. Other than the gong, soft music played in the overhead speakers in the dining room, which were the only external sounds besides life moving outside the gated community. I found myself sitting at one of a few dining room tables with four strangers. I did not know where to set my gaze. Was it rude to look at them? Was it evasive to ignore them? If I looked out and enjoyed the view, was that rude also? Where did they come from? What were their stories? Do they speak English? Did they travel long and far to be here? Are those two a couple? Are they married? Are they interested in me? Are they thinking the same about me? Should I have worn makeup? How will they know all the cool things about me? How could I find common ground with these folks?

Indeed, I was experiencing self-realization! I was realizing how egocentric I was, how much I love to turn a subject back about me and my story, what my place in the world is in-between the spaces when I meet someone new, and how much I loved to meet someone new. I realized my discomfort immediately and reminded myself why I was there. My personal intention was to rest and re-member myself. I wanted to mentally check out of the day-to-day and take advantage of lots of time to read and meditate without distractions.

Then I heard it. No sooner did I reaffirm my intention on why I was there, from the overhead speakers I heard the *Kol Nidre,* the haunting melody played only during the beginning of Yom Kippur services, the holiest of days of the Jewish year. It is the time when Jews present themselves to God for judgment of the past year's transgressions, and according to the degree of conservatism, a day of judgment and fate for the coming year. Some consider it a prayer, but it is said to be a legal and binding agreement before you and God. The music is stunning and best when played on a cello. Short of a YouTube recording, I have never heard that melody performed outside of synagogue on Yom Kippur. Yom Kippur was months away. It was as if Yogiji himself had sent it after hearing my intentions and sealed the deal after I had signed a proverbial binding contract. I looked around at the faces in the room to see if I was the only Jew because surely, any Jew would have the same expression on their face and that would not be a violation of any rules or boundaries. It turns out I was alone in my amazement. In fact, I could not share it with anyone because it was only for me. It was our sacred agreement, and it would be the first of many sublime experiences packed into five seemingly short days.

I headed back to my room uncharacteristically tired. Before too long my body started to cleanse. For hours, toxins left my body, leaving me dehydrated and exhausted. I missed dinner that night and slept for 10 hours. I awoke renewed and hungry. After breakfast, I found an oversized comfy chair in the corner of a little alcove off my room, like my own little library space. I sat down with a book, but quickly put it down and decided to practice my meditation which always included my anchoring question, "Where are you?"

I had Thomas Keating's Book *The Human Condition* in my lap and had just read about God's first question to Adam, "Where Are *You?*" (Emphasis on *You*). I asked myself that question. I then heard, "You are here, at the Hart Ashram." It was not coming from me, but the spirit of Yogiji himself standing just a few feet away. I could feel him. I could almost see him. I know he was there and with whom I carried on a conversation. Luckily, I am a prolific journaler and have copious notes because I would have doubted my memory all these years later. I was clear that the room I was in was not the Hart Ashram. "I" was the Hart Ashram. "I" was the sacred space in which I could dwell, be, and find wisdom, solace, and peace. From that day on, my anchoring statement is, "Here I am."

By the second night, I was starting to feel grounded, rested, and much more comfortable in the social setting of the dining room. Sitting over my evening meal and before I picked up my fork, I gave thanks. I thanked the omnipresent for the abundance and sustenance. I thanked those who carefully prepared the food. This was my standard blessing. Yet that night I did not stop there. I found myself in gratitude to the ones who care-fully pulled the food from the tree or out of the ground. I thanked the tree or Earth's soil for growing the food so it could end up in front of me. I thanked the food itself. Then I thanked the seed of the food who grew into its highest manifestation so it could be recirculated through me.

In Judaism, there is a prayer for just about everything, including every blade of grass that has an angel whispering in its ear, "Grow! Grow! Grow!" So, I thanked the angels who prayed for the seed to grow, so it could be care-fully gleaned, prepared, presented, and consumed by me. The responsibility of how I honor my body that is now the recipient of this seed's sacred journey, let alone savor the food itself, got really big and slightly heavy. The silence and self-realization afforded me the timefulness to slow down to the speed of gratitude.

The next morning, I sat down at the head of the table, which was the only seat left but one with a full ocean view. I noticed two new faces, a man and a woman, and began my internal inquisition. *Where did they come from? Are they are married? What's their story? Do they speak English? Are they on vacation?* My head was confused.

In my biography, I call myself a "social artist" adding, "I paint with people and love to get them all over me." I am an odd bird who loves a long subway ride. I am fascinated by people, especially the confluence of the social, economic, ethnic, and cultural tapestry in one small space, traveling together. The only thing we may all have in common is the direction and speed we are heading and that excites me. It's not unusual for an overwhelming sense of Love to cascade over me in such an environment, as best described by the Trappist monk and author Thomas Merton. In his writing, *Conjectures of a Guilty Bystander* he writes, "...I was suddenly overwhelmed with the realization that I loved all those people, that they were mine and I theirs, that we could not be alien to one another even though we were total strangers. It was like waking from a dream of separateness, of spurious self-isolation in a special world, the world of renunciation and supposed holiness… This sense of liberation from an illusory difference was such a relief and such a joy to me that I almost laughed out loud…"

The holiness of a busy subway car is not to be missed. I strongly recommend it. But one needn't be in such an environment to experience this divinity. You can be sitting in a small dining room with strangers whom you will never know, have no idea what their lives look like, or where they are coming from to fully and completely love them.

Contemplating the mysteries of it all while looking out over the treetops to Grandmother Ocean, a huge hawk sailed right in front of the window. His wingspan was stunning. Before I could exhale, he came back again as if he made a quick U-turn just to entertain us. Just like I had searched for someone who would recognize the *Kol Nidre* the night before, I turned to our table and connected with this new woman sitting diagonally from me. Our eyes met. She saw him too and seemed equally moved and thrilled. It may have only been a few seconds, but I can still feel myself being embraced by her eyes. We shared a moment of supreme awe and wonder. Her big brown eyes hugged my soul and just when I did not think my heart could get any fuller, it stretched to new limits. Now what? We just had this intimate encounter. I was not alone in this moment of enchantment. In fact, I think Yogiji was in on this one too. I had to be open to receive such a connection. There cannot be any ego or limiting beliefs to contaminate the alchemical process, whether it be on a subway car or in a community dining room.

"Look and you shall receive" was a magical spell I discovered I could cast with great ease and even greater success. I decided to put it to the test on something new. I set my intent on materializing another hawk. I decided to stroll the grounds and found a tiny sliver of grass behind an obscure gate off the parking lot between the retreat center and the temple above. There I sat alone on a worn white plastic patio chair facing the same direction as the dining room view. I could see the horizon of the blue ocean beyond the tall, aged trees. I took my seat and looked out beyond the trees, up to the sky, all the while knowing I would see this winged one I was seeking.

A hummingbird zipped by and I came close to accepting it, but then it dawned on me to be more precise in what I was looking for. After all, details matter, which is a lesson I had learned oh-so-well. I repeated my wish with clarity and emotion. I found myself in a focused meditation on the horizon. I must have gotten swept away. I have no idea how long I was there. Suddenly, my gaze pulled back from the demarcation of where the water meets the sky to that which was directly in between us. It was a hawk, sitting on the tippy-top of a tree, as if I was looking right through it but was so focused on what was beyond that I missed what was right in front of me. I kept my gaze on the hawk for what felt like 10-minutes. I took a quick glance at my watch and when I looked back, it was gone. I said, "thank you," and went to my room to take a nap.

When registering for your stay at Lake Shrine they recommend not leaving the grounds because driving or changing your environment shifts your energy and may hamper your experience. However, Rule #2 says there are no rules other than respecting silence (and some basic decorum like refraining from marital relations if you are sharing a room with your spouse). Because I consider myself something of a "beach blanket guru," I felt I could handle the 1-mile stroll to sit on the sand to pay a visit to Grandmother. To the left of where I sat was a small jetty. I watched the waves hit the rocks time and time again, yet the rocks never budged. Were they that solid in their ground and confidence that no external conditions or circumstances could rattle them? The constant barrage of waves did not stand a chance.

Water does not ask permission of the rocks it hits, blame them for being in its way, or ask what they are. The properties of water provide life, energy, nutrients, and sustainability. It is a carrier and transport, resting place, playground, and home. It has its holy work to do, and the rocks provide a place to land in a partnership of mutual respect. The rocks are also solid and stand confidently. They can take the water's hits without judgment or being moved because they know what they are.

I took a photo of the encounter which today is the background of my screensaver to remind me of the power to withstand the crashing waves that may be trying to knock me down, and to respect them for their holy work. It's amazing how helpful a simple reminder of a screensaver photo can be.

The grounds of Lake Shrine have two entrances. The upper entrance has direct access to the parking lot for the Self Realization Fellowship temple. Below, is the access to the public entrance to walk the grounds and stroll around the small lake and shrines. Between the public grounds and the temple sits the retreat center, accessible from both entrances by a coded locked gate and a set of stairs.

Walking down to the beach I noticed my knee was bothering me. I have never had knee issues before. It was not really a problem, but as I was sitting on the beach, I realized I had a big uphill walk to get back. I also realized what time it was since the public grounds on the lower lot closed at 4:30 PM. It was now 4:40.

While sitting on the sand, I contemplated the incidents that occurred thus far, and realized that if my thoughts create my reality, I could practice and prove it to myself by willing the gates to open. I had no doubt I would get through the lower gates and would not have to walk up the steepest part to the upper parking lot. I could feel the Multisensory Human condition pulsating in my veins, which created the field for intention and will to say, in unison, "Yes to the 5th power!"

I headed up the hill not thinking too hard about it and walked up the short driveway, having every intention of stepping over the threshold. As I approached the gate, I was aware there were now less than three feet between my nose and the gate. I did not hesitate. Within an inch of a collision, the massive wooden entrance gates opened. I began to walk through but had to get out of the way as a car driven by one of the monastics was driving out, having triggered the exit. Then I remembered, I still had a 152-step staircase to traverse up to the retreat center.

Nothing changes until ideas change.

~ James Hillman

Mind Over Matter to The Power of You

Sande: "Every cell in my body is vibrating, as if they are bouncing off my intestinal walls, running amuck."
Brenda: "Dear, those are your one trillion cells waiting for your direction."

When Brenda Gustin, whose PhD in Hermetic Science has served me well, bestowed upon me that simple visualization, I headed for my special chair, took a deep breath, and warmly proclaimed in an inviting and calm inner voice, *Come to Attention.* Like a mother gathering her children to her lap, within just a few minutes all were in line. The energy relaxed within a few minutes of taking command. I then realized the wisdom of the body is the soul's instrument and I was out of tune. I was not playing it with the respect and dignity it deserved; the intelligence of what my cells were collectively telling me.

In the article "The Mental Universe" by Richard Conn Henry, he states, "The 1925 discovery of quantum mechanics solved the problem of the Universe's nature. Bright physicists were again led to believe the unbelievable, this time, that the Universe is mental." Hmmm. The universe is not a machine, it's a thought. Henry goes on to say, "We have no idea what this mental nature implies, but, the great thing is, it is true." That's right. In the immortal words of Neil DeGrasse Tyson, "It's science. Whether you believe it or not, it's true."

Bruce H. Lipton PhD, cell biologist and researcher-turned-spiritual-leader bridging the two worlds, describes the moment he walked into the laboratory as a stem cell biologist with no spiritual disposition or awareness, and walked out in tears, a spiritually woke man. It was the moment he discovered that energy generated to instruct gene activation happens outside of the cell, rather than in the cell nucleus, and that energy is instructed by our thoughts that therefore become our reality. This further supports his findings that thoughts do not reside inside our heads. Like radio waves, they broadcast out to the field and rearrange the molecules to create our reality. Mind blown? If a critical mass of people (say, 100,000 in the Rose Bowl) all have the same thought at the same time, broadcasted to the (football) field, we can change the world. Global minutes of prayer hosted by peace activists have been inviting us to participate in such mass appeal since the internet provided the world with connectivity to pray together.

Since our thoughts create our cell's environment, we ought to pay honor to our thoughts and make sure they are as full of integrity as can be because they are clearly a determining factor in the collective wholeness of our bodies and our lives. In fact, learning some simple steps to regulate our nervous system is essential to give us choice in the matter so that it is informed by grace, which is critically important to our health and well-being.

On this road trip of a lifetime, we will find we need to pull over and check the engine when the warning light starts blinking. Our vagus nerve informs our Resilience System which runs our Operating Systems, and they are all running hot, requiring regulation. Our autonomic nervous system is hyper-aroused. Sensing danger, it responds by kicking in adrenaline and cortisol, resulting in fight/flight/freeze signals released through the sympathetic nervous system for our survival. While we are no longer primitive man running from tigers, our vehicle is an old model and these age-old wiring systems still serve us well.

Life University Center for Compassion and Integrity and Secular Ethics provides these three steps to regulating our nervous systems as one of the easiest fixes in their Compassionate Integrity Training:

1. **Tracking:** Notice the sensation in your body. As an observer, identify the unpleasant feeling. Where are you deregulated, feeling anxiety, or out of balance?
2. **Resourcing:** Recall a memory of when you were in a state of well-being, or even bliss. Perhaps you were holding your child in your arms for the first time and your heart felt like it would expand out of your chest, or a time when you were completely relaxed or engaged in a sport where you were in the flow. It may also be when you felt the Multisensory Human sensation. Soak in that feeling and notice what happens when your focus turns from the unpleasant sensation you were first feeling. Notice your pulse. Notice other sensations. It does not make the problem or issue go away, but it does remind you who is in charge and now you have a better chance at making

a choice that serves you well. Like my friend Brenda told me, "It's just your cells waiting for your direction."

3. **Grounding:** To complete the process of regulating the nervous system, notice your contact with the surface you are sitting, lying, or standing on and remember you are supported, especially if you are feeling "out of body."

Now your parasympathetic system is engaged and releases hormones that elicit feelings of well-being, and you can "rest and digest."

My resilience zone is the space between the ocean floor where I ground myself, and the external power of the white water rushing overhead. It's the space where I know when I am ready, I can plant my feet, rest, digest, and come up for air and make healthy, balanced choices for my next move.

Patricia Fero, in addition to being my personal cheerleader and friend, is also a psychotherapist who pointed out that 95% of brain activity is unconscious. These include habits and patterns, beliefs and values, and repressed memories. Also, 40% of behavior is habitual, taking anywhere from 15 to over 250 days to form a new habit. I'll take that 250 and bet you I can tame that habit in 28 days.

In the mid-1990's, beginning with the recognition of neuroplasticity, neuroscientists concurred that an adult brain was malleable and able to be rewired, increasing cortical thickness. Like a Mack truck driving down the same highway repeatedly, deep grooves start to form in the asphalt by repetitive motion and weight. Our thoughts may as well weigh two tons because they also wear pathways in our brains so our thoughts, especially the subliminal ones, can stream on their own without any help, like a slip-and-slide on a downward grassy hill. No need to think much, you just flip that light switch or drive the same path to work. The thought is running in the background while you are busy thinking of other things, thus, the subconscious is in charge. Do the same thing repeatedly for about 28 days, and you have a habit.

Neuroplasticity allows us to manipulate muscle memory, so the muscles automatically know what to do with little reminding, but without practice, atrophy sets in and gelatinous muscles are sure to follow.

In my early 20's, I entered the world of sales. I read everything I could about sales techniques, positive motivation and inspiration. In the back of *Success* magazine, I found the tiny article, "How to End Procrastination." The simple practice is saying these three words repeatedly 25 times, 2-3 times a day. "Do it now. Do it now. Do it now." I practiced by counting on my fingers and toes in my daily shower and each time I went into the restroom (which we do about five times a day). Before I knew it, "Do it now" would pop into my mind when I hadn't even realized I was procrastinating. What the subconscious picks up on, the habit responds to in auto-pilot. I have not procrastinated in about 40 years. I also haven't had to practice either. Those grooves are so deep and sheathed over, they are cemented into my system as solid as the Holland Tunnel. In the same way positive affirmations work (and are highly recommended), who couldn't use a cheerleader reminding us to recite, "I forgive myself for my limitations and human-ness," "We live in a conscious, loving Universe," or "I accept and love myself unconditionally." Try, "I honor myself for having said yes to the Liminal Odyssey," 25 times, five times a day.

Intentional repetition of thought and statements, and meditation are stellar ways to reprogram our operating systems and is applicable to both individuals and entire societies.

Carl Jung describes the model of Depth Psychology as exploring what lies at the core of the psyche. The top of the pyramid is the conscious mind, below that the unconscious mind, and floating in between the unconscious mind and the collective unconscious mind is the cultural unconscious. This is our connection to our tribe and kindred others. It is also our societal belief system where we take way too much for granted. That is until we question our thoughts and the default belief system of a culture we live within that lies beneath the conscience at the subconscious level. Because neuroplasticity is the understanding that adult brains can be rewired with awareness capacity-building practices like meditation and repetition, we, not our subconscious, have control. This is the same way culture works, with a collective agreement to accept the way things are, like never putting down a cell phone. We do contribute to the big culture, one trance-induced individual at a time. It's time to wake up and put the phone down from time-to-time.

As a society, we must change our collective thoughts because that is the source of the problems in our world. Yet, we are all running around like emasculated policemen chasing crazy turkeys waiting for someone else to fix the bigger problem. We must rewire society's brain. I call it rewiring the "communal neuropathways," another claim-to-fame in my book of coined expressions.

Physicists suggest that the simple act of raising your little finger in the air rearranges all the molecules in the universe. When we live into our authentic self, we make the world better just by living in our authentic power, as if to rearrange the DNA of the world towards Universal Love. We have evidence it works. Just lift your eyebrows and feel for yourself. You've also just made the world a little nicer.

Brenda showed me that every one of the 37 trillion cells in our bodies is a citizen, and each citizen has a nucleus. In each nucleus is a universe of intelligence. The energy sourced to inform our being happens outside the cell, informed by thoughts. This means that when we are the captain of our thoughts, the great thought that is the Universe also changes. So then, the only way to change the world collectively is when we collectively share the same thoughts that we believe benefit us, thus changing the mind of the Universe we collectively create. In order to be a responsible member of the collective is to be in our own integrity of our individual thoughts, because clearly those thoughts matter. We now know it's true. Just ask the dog.

While on this liminal space exploration, I came upon an article in the *Journal of the American Institute of Architects* after learning that blueprints of a home or building use the term," liminal space" when describing hallways and staircases, the thresholds between rooms and living and public spaces. I was intrigued by the symbolism of the length of the hallway with rooms to step into, or the angle of a spiral staircase depending on the lesson to learn. It made sense to dig deeper. I was not too surprised to find the liminal space's impact on a community.

In his article *The Architecture of Liminal Space*, columnist Aaron Betsky re-examines public spaces and the roles of architects and citizens in shaping them. He writes:

"My focus has been on asking the question of whether there still is some space, both physical and mental, that we share as a community or communities. The central problem, as I see it, is the privatization of space, as we wealthy few retreat into our conditioned cocoons and condense our contexts into screens, venturing outside in equally controlled environments, while millions are forced to wander a space that does not belong to them, in which they have no rights, and from which they are often excluded. In a virtual sense, our collective identities (and they are always multiple) are more and more the domain of either private entities or state organizations over which we have little control."

Before I printed Aaron's quote, I reached out to him for permission. In looking for his contact information, I found he is the Director of Virginia Tech's School of Architecture. I remembered my dear friend Christine's husband Neil is also a renowned architect, so asked if he knew Aaron. As synchronistic affairs go, Neil and Aaron were roommates, and Aaron was a guest at their wedding. Immediately, I recognized the meaningful connection as something that would drive me right into the eye of something important. I felt it in my bones and trusted something more would emerge than his permission to quote him. Dropping Neil's name in the subject line for insurance, I wrote a little introduction to *The Liminal Odyssey*. Aaron wrote me back within hours with permission. He also recommended I investigate the meaning of "heterotopia."

Heterotopia of space is described by many as an "elusive concept," which was introduced by French philosopher Michel Foucault in his 1967 lecture "Of Other Spaces." It refers to places that have meaningful connections to other places, eliciting feelings of familiarity or that identifies a condition of relativity. Think motel room, prison, gardens, shipyards. And like most, not obvious until the observer finds the relation for thoughtful inquiry in time.

Aaron introduced me to another perspective of the power of liminal space, where I see the concept of synchronicity and Kairos time relatable to more than our human experience, but to our human experience of the physical spaces we are in. And, because those are largely public spaces, they have an impact on our culture, which involves a critical mass of people with similar thoughts broadcasted out to the field.

We are truly more powerful than most of us are aware and/or leverage. We are not only architects of our lives, but of our communities and the world. Our contributions are significant. And, since we are also the captain of our 37 trillion-plus citizen cells, we are responsible for the entire crew on our Liminal Odyssey. Why wouldn't we construct the finest infrastructure of super-highways that lead to our bliss and improve the conditions for the world at the same time?

Indeed, we are the active co-architects of our society, and the control we have access to begins with the energy outside every cell. We do have control with our ideas, with our thoughts, and in the field between our cells. That requires awareness consciousness and repetitive practice. But first, we must examine our ideas and how they got planted in the first place. Drop into our liminal space, ask the questions, notice the Multisensory Human condition, question assumptions, listen intently into a condition of discovery, pay attention to will because he can be slippery, and practice, practice, practice. Then we will have made a habit of sliding into the Liminal Odyssey and ensuring a fun and successful journey. We are as powerful as we think. Think care-fully.

Imagine the outcome when we grow collectively by way of individual contribution into that cultural liminal space. It is crowd-sourcing change at its best and is the only way that is regenerative and resilient for this next era we are moving into, with or without us.

> *"The field is the sole governing agency of the particle."*
> ~ As attributed to Albert Einstein

If the field is the Universe, and the governing agency of the particle its people, yet the people's consciousness creates the field, but our thoughts are of the field, who changed its mind first, the Universe or the collective consciousness? Move over chicken and the egg, there's a new debate in town.

Eleven
Dear Linda

*In your dark days, just turn around and I will be there
and maybe I won't have any more light to give than you already have,
but I will take your hand and we will find the light together.*

~ Jim Storm

When Sally handed me Linda's yearbook to sign, I had no idea what was to come. Linda and I sat at the same pod of tables in Mr. Kulie's 5th grade class and we rode the bus together in middle school. Except for our bus route, and that we found Mr. Kulie's ankle-high boots funny, we had very little in common. She was quiet and studious, and I was neither. But I liked Linda because she laughed at my jokes. When Linda moved to New Jersey mid-schoolyear, her best friend Sally passed around her yearbook.

Sally was also studious, but way too overconfident and looked just like her Pilgrim ancestors. She never let an opportunity pass without reminding us of her heritage, like a claim to fame. Bowl cut hair, tall and thin, always neatly dressed, and chin always held high, she did not care for my humor, but invited me to sign Linda's yearbook anyway. I not only signed my name and something like, "Have a bitchen summer," I included my address. After all,

New Jersey was a world away. In retrospect, this was my first realization of a fascination with different cultures that still preoccupies my curiosity today.

It did not take long for Linda to write. In my first letter, I asked about the mysterious world of New Jersey including what kind of television shows they had. That was at the end of our 7th grade in 1973.

While I was maneuvering through the awkward and smelly world of middle school, Linda was there. As I stepped over every pebble, cried every tear, experienced every mountain and rushing river that swept me under, she was there. She helped me make life changing choices, and only once did she let me know she was disappointed with a decision I made. Even in that situation, she was my biggest advocate, supporter, and a true friend.

She was my living diary. I told her everything, and I also went through it all with her as she struggled with every challenge, mistake, rough road, joy, and celebration. She was at the end of any pen, pencil, or marker. We exchanged letters on colorful stationery, notebook paper, napkins, and even a brown paper bag because that's all I had with me, and I needed a friend. She sat with me and Grandmother Ocean, on the school bus, in my room, and later, on buses, airplanes, and in hotel rooms. Many of those letters were tear-stained. We named the long and weathered letters "purse letters" because they took so long to make it into a mailbox, only to be added to until they became short novels. She was the reason I raced home each day to check the mailbox. Then, one of my letters to her was intercepted by her mom.

That was when I first realized our letters were sacred. They were a safe place where no one could take away our authentic thoughts and feelings. There's no judgment and no editing of truths. As difficult as it was for Linda, I too felt violated that her mom read my journal.

Most letters were about a week apart, some longer. We went through everything together: fights with our siblings and parents, our crushes, friends, first loves, losing our virginity, our jobs, adventures, concerts, trips, everything. When I visited her, we spoke as if I lived around the corner. When her husband spoke of other people in their lives, I knew them all. Linda came to California to be the Maid of Honor at my wedding, and one morning years later I was awoken very early to hear the news she was pregnant with her first child.

Unlike our typical BFF, our relationship was expressed through the same process as when one journals. The depth and breadth of what came out of the pen, and later fingertips, came from a different place than on the end of a phone or in person.

It took us a long time to evolve to email. It was weird. I missed the waiting game, handwriting, and a different energy because it was in real-time. Yet, it was my persistence to make the transition. Technology had sped up the world, so why not our relationship?

From the time a letter is sealed in an envelope, the truth on paper is either not frothed with the same energy that wrote it or alchemized into some great realization we were forced to face alone. It's in that timefulness that we wait until the response appears and allow it to simmer. The realities of our world deemed it necessary, even convenient, to move to email communication. It was completely necessary for my sanity to hear from Linda as quickly as other things were emerging.

In addition to day-to-day updates, our email messages also provide opportunities to brag, pat ourselves on the head, and crown our own glory. It is because of this that I have had the gift of recognizing my successes; a seriously necessary practice and a benefit to the nervous system.

I have not had a joy or accomplishment that she has not applauded or a problem for which I haven't received sound advice, and I have been the same for her when all she needed was for me to read about her struggles with her toxic work environment. I have lived through Linda managing her own journey and ultimately ditching the toxicity, securing land, and launching a business: *My Purple Barn* lavender fields and products.

When I first realized the theory of the Liminal Odyssey, I bounced it off of Linda. When she read my theory, she did not immediately respond with the usual enthusiasm and pompoms shaking. Instead, in the form of a question, she pointed out a hole that was an invitation to look into and either clarify or fill in. Ultimately, it was neither. The hole became a tunnel that took me to places I hadn't imagined. It not only affirmed this philosophy for me, but showed me new elements that would have gone unrealized. I think about the me that would have deflated to flat and let something I found profound become full of holes. Because of her truth, told in the environment of trust, my vision was now holy. Then the parade and pompoms commenced.

Recently, I received this email from Linda: "So, thinking about your Liminal Odyssey. Tell me if this fits it. As a kid, I LOVED the galloping gourmet, Julia Child, and used to pretend I was a cook on TV. My grandmother taught me to make Scottish shortbread. I have made it for years. The kids and a few friends love it. One of the first lavender cookies I ever had was lavender shortbread. So tasty. I have wanted to sell my culinary lavender but have held back since that is another level of insurance and permits. My neighbor has a commercial food license.

Two weeks ago, I saw this adorable lavender rolling pin. I had to have it. I had no plans for it but really needed to have it. Yesterday my brother sends a text saying, "Here is an idea for you, shortbread with edible flowers." Today at the farmers' market, most of what was sold was food. I thought, gee, if I had that lavender shortbread, I could sell out. Am I living the Liminal Odyssey?

I responded, "Absolutely! The Liminal Odyssey is how you put all the pieces together and honor it. Had you not paid attention to the clues and gems and opportunities, you may have missed the massive opportunity it may become and the new big thing. I absolutely support you fully! Without a doubt do it! By the way, you have also sent me the dry ingredients of your grandmothers' recipe in a jar to put together as a gift years ago!

Love,

Sande"

Now Linda is testing out her grandmother's shortbread cookies with lavender from her field. Photos of different cookie designs are flying to me in texts for my opinion.

Herein lies my proof of concept! Linda's Liminal Odyssey started with her call to action. Something had to change because she was miserable at work. She then came to her support system (I will take a bow here) and ditched the misery and replaced it with lavender. Then she followed the threads and clues dropped decades ago with a fake studio audience in her kitchen with her grandmother over her shoulder. What's more is left to be discovered, but I, for one, know it will be extraordinary.

So that I was completely understanding the magnitude of what Linda was expressing, I wrote her for clarification. "Would you then say knowing about the Liminal Odyssey helped?" Her reply, "YUP!"

When I was 26, I visited her. She showed me a box containing all the letters I ever sent her. I was moved and embarrassed at the same time. I did not save her letters. I did not save them for the same reason she raced home to beat her mom to the mailbox. While I was aware that what I was writing was tender, vulnerable, or often incriminating, it did not stop me from feeling safe, authentic, and honest.

My 12-year-old curiosity was my call to action. I followed the tug and put my address in a yearbook. We committed to the journey together, adjusted course and have been one another's wizard, mentor, and fairy Godmother for 48+ years. We have overcome intrusive mothers and paper shortages. Gems and charms in the form of yearbooks and rolling pins have been scattered on our paths and we have picked them up and expanded and alchemized them from the mundane to the holy.

This is an Odyssey we will be on until death do us part.

Today, Linda and I text and email, sometimes daily. When I first told her I was writing this book, she said I could thank her for 48 years of practice. And I do. As I am unpacking our journey so far, Sally was my ally. I would never have guessed that on the tetherball court at Pt. Vicente Elementary School. She was as a fierce competitor, an aristocrat among 12-year-olds, and not my cup of tea, but I bow to her today for asking me to sign Linda's yearbook.

"Twenty years from now you will be more disappointed by the things you didn't do than by the ones you did do. So throw off the bowlines! Sail away from safe harbor. Catch the trade winds in your sails."

- Mark Twain

Fulfilling Our Planetary Assignment with Courage

Because of the habit I formed of paying attention to clues and gems, as well as living in my integrity to make sure credit is paid where credit is due, I can easily go back prior to June 6th, 1982 to see the unorthodox response to something even nuttier and more dangerous than putting my address in a yearbook; something that catapulted me into this life of adventure and began with a courageous Yes, inspired by curiosity, not unlike the culture in the faraway land of New Jersey.

After a long day at the beach, my friend Cindy and I took a shortcut through an alley to her car parked behind a shopping center. We came upon three men moving into an apartment. They were older by about 10 years and looked completely harmless.

Always up for an adventure, we hung out for a while in the alley until John, a sales manager for a new radio station playing New Wave music and whose buddies were helping him move, asked if we wanted to earn some cash. This is the part of the story where you are screaming out loud, "Run!" We didn't run. I wanted to follow this adventure and we ended up returning to unpack and alphabetize about 3,000 record albums, and we got to keep the duplicates. I was then offered a job to clean his apartment after school and walk his teeny, aptly named dog Blinken.

I had a key to his apartment, which was also a refuge by the beach since he was never home. I don't think I saw him but once or twice in the year I was his dog walker/housekeeper. He paid me well and usually left me concert tickets. One day he left me four tickets to Peace Sunday at the Rose Bowl. I would never have gone otherwise.

It was not until I was well into writing this book that I shared this story with Charlon, my editor. I put a big exclamation mark at end of my story with, "Saying yes to these three men in an alley was such a stupid thing to do." Her response was, "Or was it? How else would those tickets to Peace Sunday end up in your hands? How else would you have heard the call that catalyzed 100,000 people to share a common thought that was meaningful to all?"

I would not have a story to tell, nor have started and stopped writing a book about Peace Sunday for the past 15 years, until this story found its rightful home, with the right purpose, and in such a curious and exciting unfolding that I continue to be amazed by today and will for the rest of my life. At some level, a certain trusting intelligence kicked in instead of the primal instinct to run. Indeed, that Yes was courageous and wise, just like the great architect, Universal Wisdom, had ordered.

When courage is engaged, we can feel it in our body. The condition typically comes in a setting where there's a need to change and chances are, a solution is already in the creative stages. My wheels tend to turn automatically where I needn't rev my engine. I hear the call and lunge. But I was not always that confident and had to learn the joy of coloring outside the lines. We have been conditioned into valuing the praise when we neatly colored in someone else's picture. And that's such a sad thing. I love it when I hear my daughter encouraging her son to be bold and create his own masterpiece… as long as it's not on the living room wall.

In 2015, I attended a women's symposium where we sat in circle, not my first or last with Jean Shinoda Bolen. She posed the dialogue prompt that would shift the trajectory of my life: (Paraphrasing) "What prevents you from answering your planetary assignment?" Simply having been asked the question and provided a safe container to answer, showed me that I did not have the confidence in my own gifts and talents. I asked myself, *Why?* and came up with nothing that held water. Expected to proclaim it to the circle meant I could not brush over it. I had to face it and I came up with no good excuse.

I could also feel my soul lighting up, as if her face was being seen and her voice heard for the first time in this lifetime. That day a seed was birthed in me that would result in dreaming up, creating, and directing the Women and Girls sector for the International Charter for Compassion organization. It was that body of work that led to relationships which resulted in, among many other experiences, trips to Japan, then Poland to work on a project at Auschwitz.

I have no doubt that without the simple question, and the right environment to answer it in, I would only have half the stories to write, a fraction of lines to connect, and pearls to explore. I would not have taken an expedition to the depths of my soul, let alone discovered a title for this book. I am even more confident there would not be a book worth writing. That seed also has a forest full of possibilities coded within it that I am entrusted with as the sacred gardener. While seemingly impossible, all I can do is lunge forward and say, "Yes."

I can see my angels collapsing into their angel chaise lounges, relieved that I am finally getting this.

We are on this Earth walk to create first-time masterpieces and we are all equipped to do that. It just takes a little sacred listening, trust, recognizing our allies in every shape and form, welcoming our fear at the door, and calling up the courage to lose our head, if we must. There's lots to learn in the fear. It's there to protect us. This is where body awareness is our best ally.

Fear will paralyze our genius. Love will set it free. We can come to that conclusion when we step into the liminal space and survey the landscape. Pull it apart and ask, "Why?" and, if we have been practicing our mantras, we can recall the gratitude for being on this Liminal Odyssey with ease and joy.

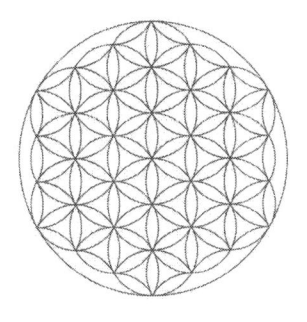

Twelve
Acorn Rain in Birkenau

They thought they buried us. They did not know we were seeds.

~ Greek poet Dinos Christianopoulos

Apparently, Grandmother Fuji was holding more secrets. In Her presence, I not only picked up a gift of vital importance of the 5th dimension, but also my next ally. This time a crone by the name Dr. Nina Meyerhof would take my hand, leading me all the way to Poland to pick up a seed, which was my next clue.

My favorite part of traveling to faraway places are the conversations I have with strangers in the seat next to me on a train, or who land next to me on a bench to take a break at an international conference. It is there where I typically meet my next inspiration, mentor, or best friend. Nina was one of the other guests of the Saionji family on our trip to Japan. As I was climbing into the group's luxury bus on our way to the United Nations University for a symposium, I was looking for someone whom I hadn't yet had a chance to meet on this trip. I looked down and Nina was patting the seat next to her like a Bubby's warm invitation.

It did not take long to fall in love with her, her admirable life's work, and her vision for an institute for peace education adjacent to the grounds at Auschwitz. Before I knew it, I was part of the One Humanity Institute team and within a few months, found myself boarding a plane to Poland.

There I would find another astounding assemblage of peace educators, politicians, activists, a major motion picture film producer, and another adventure with Sally Ranney, also in Japan, whose vision for an environmentally sustainable compound was essential to this project. We spent nearly a week together, exploring the possibilities of this initiative, and the town of Oświecim (the Polish name for Auschwitz).

On our second day, we headed for the Auschwitz-Birkenau State Museum on the site of the Auschwitz concentration camp. We were chatting away on the bus, and my gaze caught railroad tracks below my window. Suddenly the entire energy of the bus dropped to solemn as we made a hard right into the parking lot, lined with weeping willows, planted after the camp was liberated.

I took one step beyond those infamous gates with the ironwork lettering that reads "Arbeit Macht Frei" (Work Shall Set You Free), and the first thing I noticed were the trees lining the road, like prisoners standing silently at attention. Thousands of people pass by every day, possibly never noticing them at all.

I could not take my eyes off of them, let alone pay attention to the tour guide. I quietly stepped aside and wrapped my arms around one of the trees and tried to listen. They didn't appear to be very old, certainly not 80+ years old. Throughout our nearly full day at both Auschwitz and Birkenau, I noticed every tree, wondering how old they were, what they witnessed, and what secrets and horrors they would hold forever in their trunks, branches, and roots. What sorrow did each tree cry out of its leaves and branches? Did they hear the sound of the orchestra of inmate musicians who were ordered to play for the pleasure of the soldiers and on the death marches to the gas chambers and selection?

Viktor Frankl is, by far the most famous of survivors of the Holocaust. In his book *Man's Search for Meaning,* he states he and other prisoners had to make a moral choice to submit internally or find meaning in their lives, giving them strength and the will to survive.

Depleted from what we had seen so far, Nina and I sat down on a small wall. I then realized; it was likely this was the same place Mr. Frankl himself once sat. Could I feel his strength? Could I muster the same capacity to find meaning in my life in such a situation? We were not even an hour into this tour, and I was wondering how I could go on.

The end of our tour consisted of visiting the memorial monuments at the back end of Birkenau, the adjacent death camp to Auschwitz, just past the burnt down building that was the crematorium where bodies were incinerated, then ashes disposed of in the nearby river. There I saw the most magnificent oak tree, a presence of nobility anchoring the far end of this large open park area.

She was at least 100 years old. And there she stood, regal yet humble, as if she were patiently waiting, waiting for someone to notice her pain. I broke free from the group and slowly approached this grandmother of a tree with reverence. After asking permission, I laid on a big hug, my arms barely reaching around a fraction of her trunk. I took a deep breath, and suddenly I heard what I thought were raindrops around me. I looked down and found I was being sprinkled with acorns. I took her gesture as a resounding, "thank you," and tucked a single acorn into my pocket.

The next morning while on an early morning jet lag stroll near my hotel, just two miles from the death camps and a hundred yards from a cow grazing in a small front yard, I stopped in the middle of a picturesque walking bridge over a narrow river lined with trees that seemed to be pregnant with life. I wondered if this is where Jews may have hidden. How long could someone live here undetected? Two ducks floated toward me, and the rich greenery was stunning. Everywhere I went in this small town of Oświęcim I wondered where Jews may have hid or been hidden. In every church I stopped in, I wondered if the wood panels on the walls were façades that covered up spaces of refuge and shelter. Did that bakery have an attic that was occupied by families for months or years?

The Liminal Odyssey

As soon as I realized the river I was standing over was the same river where ashes were disposed of by the Nazis to hide their "evidence" it occurred to me that those ashes must have been fertilizing all the trees and plants lining this little river, absorbing those souls. If I was curious if those trees were once refuge for Jews, I had no doubt now. They were now homes, teeming with life-giving nutrients, oxygen, and sustainability for all the creatures.

I became overwhelmed with a sense of life, a fullness, and reverence for the sanctity of life, and with a certain grace of forgiveness. I was surprised because I should have been saddened by this realization. Why wasn't my heart heavy? I looked deep into the trees and plants. I looked carefully at where the water met the dense greenery. I saw the faces of millions of prisoners. Then, I heard, *We choose Love*. As clear as the blue sky, I heard, *Of course, We Choose Love*. Then I felt the sentiment, *Mourning does not serve the memory of all of us who perished. It is your job to Love mercifully because we cannot. Love is all that matters. Love is all there is. Of course, We Choose Love.*

If you cannot change a situation,
we are challenged to change ourselves.

~ Viktor Frankl

Being The Sacred Gardener

When we look at what is before us, we are gifted the privilege to ask ourselves, what is the story, lesson, or treasure between the seams? Trust is to let go of the perceived idea of what is before us and simply assume there is a crevasse to see the light through, even if it requires pliers to pull it apart, or maybe a well-aimed hammer strike. We can know there is a priceless gem waiting to be found inside, and each element of the gem is a prism of deep, rich shades, and sometimes unrecognizable colors that dazzle and amaze the senses. Each experience contains a magical story and potential with rippling effects to spark hearts, imaginations, and wild creativity of everyone on the planet.

If Viktor Frankl could embody this belief amidst suffering the horrors of a Nazi concentration camp, I can muster up the courage to know it's alive inside of a heartbreaking punch to the stomach.

I am going to guess that Mr. Frankl may have had the disposition of a positive thinker but, come on! The internal steel cabling he walked out of that camp with was practiced, tried to an unimaginable extreme, and proven. He endured three years, 24/7 of big T-trauma which became his research and practice. Daily he carried a chisel to crack open his eyes and heart to the nature of possibility. After all, we change ourselves by changing our minds. As a prisoner, he had a choice, and he chose freedom.

The Seed In Our Pocket

A single oak tree can produce approximately 10,000 acorns a year, each with a potential to grow and drop 10,000 more. And those 10,000 will each possibly drop 10,000 and so on. Imagine just one tree's purposeful existence and the lives it alone impacts. From critters, bird nests, shade, impact on weather patterns, to each putting 260 pounds of oxygen in the air and removing 2.6 tons of carbon dioxide each year. That's a potential life well-lived nestled in my pocket.

A seed that lies underground, teeming with possibilities, must first disintegrate so new life can emerge and fulfill its own master plan. Of course, not all seeds will make their way to being planted, yet the power of one little seed resting in my pocket knows something I don't. Its wisdom is coded into it with big plans. When I hold the seed (or oak embryo) I can almost feel its pulse. If every blade of grass can have an angel praying over it, so must this future forest in the palm of my hand.

What is my responsibility to care for it, the offspring of this magnificent and traumatized Grandmother Oak? My Mother/Crone was in full activation with a fierce determination. What potential am I coded with and what can this seed teach me? I made a solemn promise to honor her and her past seven generations of life somehow, as if my next seven generations depend on it. I was given the gift and the awesome responsibility to be the sacred gardener of one acorn that I slipped into my pocket at Birkenau. I was at the place of resurrection and a sacred call to action simultaneously.

A forest of potentiality lies within each of us. It is my crystal-clear prayer that the Liminal Odyssey supports us to be the sacred gardener of our life manifesting in bliss.

We must let go of the life we have planned, so as to accept the one that is waiting for us. Find a place inside where there's joy, and the joy will burn out the pain. Follow your bliss and the universe will open doors where there were only walls.

-Joseph Campbell

Epilogue

Everyone has a story. Actually, everyone has a universe of stories waiting to be discovered. I'd challenge they are all miraculous.

I originally set out to tell one story 15 years ago about an experience I once had at a no-nukes rally. I continued to put it down because the timing was not right. I thought it was writer's block, but looking back I can clearly see I simply hadn't yet been gifted the tools to navigate what more wanted to be lived and told. It became the seed in my pocket. While I was not cognitively aware of it at the time, somehow, I had to have known it would birth a forest of other stories waiting to be revealed. A few of those stories revealed themselves during the writing of this book. I have shared those intimate details with you in real-time. In that way, you have been my ally, and for that I am so grateful.

I have always known I was born with an innate sense of responsibility to expand every opportunity to its fullest potential. I knew there was something more to my story. I just did not know the sheer magnitude and depth of what was possible until I noticed the threads and patterns, allies, and lessons. As I began to compile them to share them with you, I found each could be attributed to a method, tool, skill, or philosophy I had learned over time.

I don't know what more there is to come on my Liminal Odyssey, but I do know I am ready for it. I am also not complete in gathering tools from others and insight on my own accord, and that anticipation is growing.

More than a few times during the writing of this book, I forgot who I was. On one occasion, I found myself in the depths of discontent, sadness, and even despair. After I picked myself up off the floor, I did what I typically do and sat back down, closed my eyes, and took a breath. I immediately re-membered and grounded myself in what I was doing. I was writing a book about this very moment so I would be the ultimate hypocrite if I did not practice it. I felt accountable to not only my soul, my angels, but to you. In that one minute, my despair was replaced with timeless joy and gratitude.

The Liminal Odyssey is a trip of a lifetime and, before we know it, we are seeing new opportunities to slow down and notice the thresholds that are welcoming invitations. The more we do, the more time we seem to have to make conscious choices as to how we respond or make sense of what's at our feet.

The origination of the game Chutes and Ladders was intended to be more than a game, but a lesson in morality, where the progression up the board represents a Hero's journey complicated by virtues in the form of ladder rungs and vices depicted as snakes. When we experience each rung as an opportunity, the sensation is that of bliss, grounded in responsibility. So, "follow your bliss" is good advice.

We are all being called on, in one way or the other, to be prepared for the emerging shift of consciousness, for our very survival. The ultimate responsibility is that we step into, not over the rungs, or thresholds, so when we do take that leap, we are in our integrity, and ultimately in our bliss.

If you close this book with the realization that your stories deserve recognition and expansion, and you are willing to apply the Liminal Odyssey, I trust the synchronicities will multiply and your awareness will heighten to a surprising degree. If your Odyssey reminds you to sink down when you are tousled in the white water, to where you can find the ground, take a breath, and have agency over what comes next, my soul, as well as yours, will rejoice.

A Note from the Editor

While I am a naturally curious person, what the Liminal Odyssey shows me, based on its ever-expanding nature, is far more interesting, and ultimately gratifying, than my need to know what's ahead. I find myself way more curious about what will be revealed in the absence or insistence of my need to know.

The in-between is where life's most potent insights, learnings and growth lie. The Liminal Odyssey is the splay of all those rich moments, a luscious a field of vastness.

You can trust the invitation of this grand adventure. It contains its own wisdom, its own flow, and its own rhythm to guide you. Your reverence and curiosity are the invitation for the petals of the Liminal Odyssey to endlessly blossom before you toward a life of celebration and dedication to the mysterious and magical unfoldment process.

Sande has gone before. With the publication of this "master opus," in the words of Dr. Nina Meyerhof, EdD, in the Foreword, she introduces the terminology and concept of a Liminal Odyssey, and provides relatable, real-world examples from her own living of its in-between influences. With this information and the frequency wave on which it is incoming, each of us is now equipped to explore and apply it to our own worlds where it means the most and has the greatest impact as we live and explore these fresh discoveries.

Cheers to breathing alive your personal Liminal Odyssey through every in-between!

~ Charlon Bobo

A Reference Guide

The 12 skills I have shared are building blocks upon the others. They are interdependent and mutually supportive. The following is a quick reference of the 12 skills outlined throughout this book. Please make sure you take stock of the skills you already know and include them in this list.

The Sacred Art of Listening invites us into the depths of our inner-most essence to welcome information for disclosure and discovery. It's in that discovery that we open new pathways for understanding and reverence for what or who is in front of us. It is possibly one of the greatest gifts we can give to ourselves and to others. As we pay attention to the stages of what each scenario represents, we can utilize this skill to pay honor to what more wants to emerge, be said, or recognized, and then trust everything happens for us.

Timefulness asks us to recognize the potency in a moment. As our society speeds up, so does our response to it. Are we skipping right over the colors, smells, textures, and possibilities that are there for us to savor and enjoy? Stay inside that moment and look around. Take some time in the fullness of the space so that our next move is thought-full and care-full because you were time-full. This realization can turn one minute into a timeless experience.

Forgiveness, Sacrifice and Bliss Recognizing if a victim mentality may be at play and replacing it with gratitude is the fast way to alchemize the experience. That experience then becomes sacred. The root word of sacrifice is *sacer*, which means *holy*. It will not surprise you that it shares the same root as the word sacred. To sacrifice something means to destroy or surrender something for the sake of something else. Too often we associate its meaning with death. And that's okay, because from death comes life. All experiences and systems that appear to dominate and yank us away from our gratitude are our gifts and opportunities to navigate, including patriarchy and consumerism.

As building blocks of capacity-building, listening and being timeful give us a chance at redefining sacrifice for the prize of bliss. Just like the acorn, it has to dis-integrate so that it can manifest its highest potential.

We Are Nature Our relationship to our natural world. Since the Agrarian Age, humans have assumed the role of dominion over our planet. Because of that, our relationship to and with nature has largely been socialized out of the Western world. The same is true for the disconnect with the nature of our own bodies. Through patterns and life-giving nutrients, nature is speaking to and for us. Not-so-subtle are the signs and symbols the nature of our body is constantly broadcasting. It's as critical to listen to one as it is the other. They both exist on our behalf to get us closer to bliss.

Sacred Cultivation of Synchronicities Our lives exist in stories; each one threaded together from the one before it, so it's natural we are going to see a meaningful coincidence from time to time, or an unlikely experience that has meaning to another chance occurrence. They happen all the time and yet we are likely to miss them if we are not paying attention. What is discovered could be an extraordinary treasure, lesson, or sign. It's my belief that those treasures are intended to be found to live our fullest life and answer our life's big questions. I also think we do ourselves a great disservice to live this life without them. The more we pay attention and pay them reverence, the more we see them in shapes and sizes that dazzle the senses and surprise us. Who would choose to miss that?

Meeting the Maiden, Mother, Crone Archetypes are avatars; inherent characteristics to encompass the particular and full expression of an individual. They are a summation of a personality type. For the purpose of making my point in this book, the Maiden/Mother/Crone are conditions and personalities of a woman's life yet can also be relatable to men. What matters here is we all pay attention to the personality in the captain's chair at any given moment. Someone's always driving the ship. Identifying if the most appropriate driver has taken the wheel is important for self-realization, to make sure we arrive safely in one piece and in our authenticity and integrity.

Impeccability and Grace Possibly the most accurate test to measure how we score on the impeccability meter is to be mind-full of our words and actions.

Are we saying what we truly mean? Forget being honest with others, because let's assume we always are, but being honest with our self is the question. This is not the book to get a lecture on the virtues of honesty, but a tiptoe through the garden of our own life to see if there are any weeds crowding the soil. Think of those weeds as toxins, poisons dangerous to our soul. We do not serve anyone, especially ourselves, if we are not authentic and our words and thoughts alike do not align with what is true for us. If we are serious about a life-well-lived, why waste a second not being fully who we are? I wrote this book with the understanding that we, as a civilization, are evolving into a new era, and each of us plays a vital role in how we get there. It's happening with or without us, and I, for one, want to be clean and impeccably dressed for the Odyssey.

The Trust Frequency Everything happens for us. Love is all there is, whether we trust it or not. The Universe is always conspiring on our behalf and the Trust Frequency is getting louder and stronger because it knows something we do not. I'd like to think it knows there's a leap in evolution coming, if not already in the works, and trust is required for that transformation. It's simply nature bringing what needs to happen to get us closer to realizing bliss. The question is, can we trust it? It's comforting to remember Step 10; The Trust Frequency, is available to anyone, anywhere, anytime.

Intergenerational Healing Awareness; Our Ancestors, Allies, and Angels Whether or not one believes in the concept of angels, there's no denying we all have ancestors. And, odds are, some of them had baggage they left for us to unpack. That baggage, just like an heirloom piece of jewelry, is ours to hold until we recognize it, discern if it's of value, and then either wear it or address it. In the end, addressing ancestral trauma may be the most important thing we can do to free our soul. Let's assume it's our divine assignment and this is our angel's top priority. For me, my belief in angels is also an exercise in humility and vulnerability. I don't know what I don't know and there's no way of proving or disproving angels. As long as they serve me as well as they do, I am really comfortable maintaining an entire army of angels. (Including a few of them who are wearing plastic disguise glasses with bushy eyebrows and mustaches, reminding me to lighten up.)

Mind Over Matter to The Power of You Unlike nature, we have rightful dominion over our minds. Awareness of the nature of our thoughts bestows upon us the power and the responsibility to govern them with care and integrity. This gives us freedom and agency to develop healthy habits if we are willing to take responsibility and practice. Then we literally can "go confidently in the direction of our dreams" and "live the life we imagine."

Fulfilling Our Planetary Assignment with Courage Each of us is gifted, like the unicorn with rare qualities and attributes that are a piece of the universal puzzle. When we conform to who we are supposed to be according to social norms, we are not showing up with that part of us that has been moving and growing in us, is a force to acknowledge, and a commitment to fulfill. We can find those qualities readily in the spaces in-between. If courage means to honor such an assignment, then follow the bliss of living our life, and row, row, row our own boat in that direction with courage, ease and grace is great advice.

Being The Sacred Gardener We have each been entrusted, by our soul's purpose, to hold a seed in the palm of our hand. That seed was given to us in the most sacred manner so that we can carry out our divine assignment. It came in the same container that has been growing in us since birth and when we plant and nurture it, we are giving it life. That seed is encoded with the intelligence of everything that will come from it, so our job is to care for it with the most delicate of intentions and will of all the lessons, skills, awareness, and love we possess.

For more information about upcoming workshops, appearances, publications, images and the Liminal Odyssey Book Club Circle Guide, complete with dialogue and journal prompts visit
www.LiminalOdyssey.com

Chapter Symbols

Chapter 1 Cho ku rei – Reiki- The Energy of the Universe

Chapter 2 - Celtics Grandmother's Knot

Chapter 3 Om- Represents the sound of the universe

Chapter 4 Asase Ye Duru- Adinkra symbol that represents power, divinity, providence, and importance of Mother Earth for human life.

Chapter 5 Greek Symbol for Psychology

Chapter 6 Triple Goddess: Maiden Mother, Crone

Chapter 7 Ma: Japanese Symbol for Empty Space

Chapter 8 Triquetra: Japanese and Celtic Symbol of the Trilogy

Chapter 9 Triskelion: Celtic Symbol of Cycles

Chapter 10 Mindfulness: a physical representation of the present moment

Chapter 11 Infinity of Friendship

Chapter 12 Flower of Life: Sacred Geometry
The pattern found in all things

References

Bolen, Jean Shinoda: Tao of Phycology, Urgent Message From Mother, Crones Don't Whine, Goddess in Every Woman www.JeanBolen.com
Bruce, Dr. H. Lipton, PhD www.BruceLipton.com
Campbell, Joseph: The Hero of a Thousand Faces and The Power of Myth with Bill Moyers www.JCF.org
The Center for Partnership Studies www.CenterforPartnership.org
Charter For Compassion www.CharterforCompassion.org
Connie Baxter Marlow and Andrew Cameron Bailey: The Trust Frequency: 10 Assumptions for a New Paradigm www.TheTrustFrequency.net
   The Conscious Loving Universe: A Guidebook (Free e-book) https://TheTrustFrequency.net/CLU-ebook.
The Dance of Souls: The Relationship https://TheTrustFrequency.net/The-Dance-of-Souls.
Eisler, Dr. Riane: The Chalice and The Blade, Sacred Pleasure, The Real Wealth of Nations www.RianeEisler.com
Gary Zukav: Seat of The Soul, Universal Human www.SeatoftheSoul.com
Center for Compassion, Integrity and Secular Ethics: http://www.compassion.life.edu
Doty, Dr. James: Into The Magic Shop www.IntoTheMagicShop.com
Dryer, Dr. Wayne: You'll See It When You Believe It www.WayneDyer.com
Fero, Patricia www.Patriciafero.com
Firestone, Rabbi, Dr. Tirzah: Wounds Into Wisdom: Healing Intergenerational Jewish Trauma www.TirzahFirestone.com
Frankl, Viktor: Man's Search for Meaning
Grandmother Flordemayo www.GrandmotherFlordemayo.com and www.FollowTheGoldenPath.org

Great Grandmother Mary Lyons www.Rainbowofbeing.wordpress.com

Hopkins, Misa: The Root of All Healing, and The Sacred Feminine Awakening series www.MisaHopkins.com

Keating, Father Thomas: The Human Condition www.ContemplativeOutreach.org/fr-Thomas-Keating/

Leadership Lessons From The Dancing Guy video- YouTube https://www.youtube.com/watch?v=hO8MwBZl-Vc

Lindahl, Kay: The Sacred Art of Listening– www.SacredListening.com

Merton, Thomas: Conjectures of a Guilty Bystander

Pagans In The Promised Land by Steven T. Newcomb

The Doctrine of Discovery, Unmasking The Domination Code https://vimeo.com/ondemand/dominationcode

The Pluralism Project www.Pluralism.org/dr-diana-eck

Ruiz, don Miguel: The Four Agreements www.MiguelRuiz.com

Sacred Circles: A Guide to Creating Your Own Women's Spirituality Group

S.A.R.A.H. (The Spiritual And Religious Alliance for Hope) www.SARAH4Hope.org

Skaggs, Katherine: Artist, Shaman Healer Sage www.KatherineSkaggs.com

The Burning Times- Documentary, Directed by Donna Reed

The Center For Compassion and Altruism Research Education (CCARE) http://CCARE.Stanford.edu

The Saionji Family: Byakko Shinko Kai www.byakko.org

Goi Peace Foundation www.GoiPeace.or.jp/en/

The Divine Spark In https://divinesparkin.jimdofree.com/

Walsch, Neale Donald: Conversations with God 1, 2 and 3 www.nealedonaldwalsch.com

Yoganando, Paramahansa: Autobiography of a Yogi www.Yogananda.org

About the Author

Sande is a mother, grandmother, wife, aunt, and sister from the steep seaside cliffs in Southern California. She is an award-winning leader in the fields of women's empowerment and interfaith community building. She founded the women's interfaith grassroots international organization S.A.R.A.H. (The Spiritual And Religious Alliance for Hope) the morning of 911, an instinct to gather women of diverse faiths to protect all that they consider sacred, now in its 19th year. Sande is actively engaged in leadership in the peace, interfaith, compassion, community building and women's empowerment sectors. Sande serves on the Women's Task Force for The Parliament of The World's Religions and founded and served as Director for the international organization The Charter For Compassion's Women and Girls sector. She served as Chair for the United Religions Initiative for North America and is also the Founder of Compassionate California, which recently became established into law by the governor's office as the first Compassionate State in the world. Sande has conducted countless workshops and produced major and smaller events in more than seven countries, presented on panels in universities, global and local organizations, and city and state level institutions. Sande is currently being inducted into the Women's Oral History Archives for Claremont Colleges in California. Sande will barter for chocolate.

Made in United States
Orlando, FL
04 March 2022